THE CIVILIZATION OF THE AMERICAN INDIAN SERIES

THE AZTECS

PEOPLE OF THE SUN

Tonatiuh (*Codex Borgia* 71).

ALFONSO CASO

THE AZTECS

PEOPLE OF THE SUN

Illustrated by MIGUEL COVARRUBIAS

Translated by Lowell Dunham

NORMAN : UNIVERSITY OF OKLAHOMA PRESS

By ALFONSO CASO:

El teocalli de la guerra sagrada. Mexico, Talleres Gráficos de la Nación, 1927.

Las estelas zapotecas. Mexico, Talleres Gráficos de la Nación, 1928.

Las exploraciones en Monte Albán temporada, 1931–32. Mexico, Imprenta Mundial, 1932.

Las exploraciones en Monte Albán temporada, 1934–35. Tacubaya, D.F., 1935.

Exploraciones en Mitla, 1934–35. (With D. F. Rubin de la Borbolla.) Mexico, Talleres Gráficos de la ofi. de pubs. y de la S. a. y f., 1936.

Exploraciones in Oaxaca . . . 1936–37. Tacubaya, D.F., Impreso de la Cultura, n.d.

Thirteen Masterpieces of Mexican Archaeology. Tr. by Edith Mackie and Jorge R. Acosta. Mexico, Editoriales Cultura y Polis, 1938.

Culturas mixteca y zapoteca. Mexico, Ediciones Encuadernables el Nacional (Biblioteca del Maestro), 1942.

La religión de los aztecas. Mexico, Imprenta Mudial, 1936; Secretaría de Educación Pública, 1945.

El pueblo del Sol. Mexico, Fondo de Cultura Económica, 1954.

The Aztecs: People of the Sun. Tr. of *El pueblo del Sol* by Lowell Dunham. Norman, University of Oklahoma Press, 1958.

INTERNATIONAL STANDARD BOOK NUMBER: 0–8061–0414–7
LIBRARY OF CONGRESS CATALOG CARD NUMBER: 58–11603

CONTENTS

ILLUSTRATIONS

PHOTOGRAPHS

(following page 97)

TRANSLATOR'S
ACKNOWLEDGMENTS

I AM especially indebted to my wife, Frances, without whose assistance I could not have made this translation in its final form; to my colleague, Antonio de la Torre, for help on difficult passages; to my good friends Stephan and Susie Borhegyi for their critical reading of the manuscript and their counsel in archaeological matters and terminology; and to Samuel Martí, Mexico City, for his suggestions.

Lowell Dunham

Norman, Oklahoma

TRANSLATOR'S INTRODUCTION

THE STORY of the Aztecs' rise from a nomadic tribe of Nahuatl-speaking Indians to become the conquerors of the Valley of Mexico and the proud possessors of one of the New World's three indigenous civilizations is an important segment of a vast American epic: the arrival of the first man on the American continent and his progress, and that of his successors, in creating a culture and ultimately a highly developed civilization. Part of the Aztec story belongs to pre-history and part of it to relatively modern history.

Some time in the dim past—the most accurate estimates place it anywhere from fifteen to twenty-five thousand years ago—men of the Mongoloid race, in search of food, made their way across the frozen Bering Strait from Asia to the North American continent. Hunting and fishing in small bands, they spread out over North America, pushing their way down into Central America, and farther down into South America until they occupied both continents in varying degrees of population density.

By the time the white man arrived in the New World, he found a wide variety of social patterns and customs in evidence among these peoples, whom he mistakenly called Indians. These patterns ranged from crude, primitive societies to those capable of observing the movements of the heavenly bodies with more precision than the Europeans who came to these shores.

But it was not until relatively recent times that anthropologists, archaeologists, and historians began to talk of Indian civilizations. Men like Means, Morley, Kidder, Vaillant, Thompson, Spinden, Maudslay, Caso, and a host of other eminent scientists and scholars have accumulated a vast amount of knowledge from excavations and studies, especially the accounts of the early Spanish missionaries in the New World.

From this body of knowledge a pattern emerged, and historians and philosophers began to speak of the Aztec civilization, the Maya civilization, and the Inca civilization. Historians and philosophers could no longer ignore America and its three indigenous world outlooks, as Hegel had done.

xiii

What made it possible for these three great civilizations to emerge —the Aztec in the Valley of Mexico, the Maya in Guatemala, Honduras, and Yucatán, and the Inca in Peru and Bolivia? In each case the domestication of a staple food supply seems to have been a deciding factor; among the Aztecs and Mayas it was maize or corn and among the Incas the white potato.

The scene of the Aztec triumph was the Central Valley of Mexico. Several centuries before Christ, agricultural tribes had already settled here, and by the time of Christ had established their great religious center at Teotihuacán. Archaeologists place the advent, rise, and fall of this great civilization roughly from the second century to the tenth century A.D. About this time a new group moved into the Valley and settled at Tula, Hidalgo. They are known to us as the Toltecs. These Indians belonged to Nahua group and seem to have come from the north or northwest into the Valley. Soon their culture and artistry spread to many parts of Mexico, reaching even as far as Yucatán and other Maya areas. However, as early as the eleventh century A.D., another related tribal group, the Chichimecs, were already in contact with the Toltecs, and by the thirteenth century they had gradually replaced the Toltecs as the dominant tribal group in the Valley.

The Aztecs were among the last of the tribes to enter the Valley. They, too, were of the Nahua group. The tribal records of the Tenochca Aztecs indicate that they began their wanderings in A.D. 1168, coming down from their legendary home in Aztlán, referred to as the "Seven Caves," or the "Place of Reeds." Evidence seems to indicate that the Aztecs, "the Crane People," migrated from the north and northwest, passing through Michoacán. Linguistically speaking, they were allied to the North American Shoshonis and to the Michoacán Tarascans. They arrived in the central valley and asked for permission to settle at Chapultepec in 1248. For some years they appear to have been almost enslaved by other tribes of the Nahua race. By the fourteenth century they had made two settlements on the islands in the lakes, one at Tenochtitlán, now called Mexico City, whose traditional founding date is given as 1325, and another at Tlaltetalco. By the fifteenth century, Tenochtitlán had become the center of Aztec growth, conquest, and expansion. The great struggle for prisoners of war had been initiated.

As early as the beginning of the sixteenth century, the Aztec capital, Tenochtitlán, dominated all other cities and had reached the height of its power and magnificence.

In 1519, the first white men, the Spaniards, under the leadership of Hernán Cortés pushed their way into the Valley of Mexico and looked with wonder and amazement upon the Aztec capital as it glittered in the high, thin mountain air. The date was November 8, 1519, according to one of Cortés' lieutenants, Bernal Díaz del Castillo. Old Bernal Díaz, some forty years later, recorded his impressions of the first view of the approach to the city:

> During the morning, we arrived at a broad causeway and continued our march toward Iztapalapa, and when we saw so many cities and villages built into the water and other great towns on dry land and that straight and level causeway going toward Mexico, we were amazed and said that it was like the enchantments they tell us of in the legend of Amadis, on account of the great towers and *cues* and buildings arising from the water and all built of masonry. And some of our soldiers even asked whether the things we saw were not a dream.[1]

The amazement of the Spaniards increased as they entered the city and were received with true regal splendor by the Emperor Moctezuma in full regalia. But it was a sad event, for the Aztecs' way of life was no longer to follow its own course. An alien world had come to impose its views upon these people and their civilization. Had the Aztec destiny run its course? The answer belongs to speculation, not to history. But the dominance of these people in the Valley of Mexico was henceforth delimited by the dates 1325 and 1519.

What was the impelling force that drove these Indians to become the masters of a great part of Central America, to develop a civilization *sui generis,* unique among the peoples of the world? One word may best answer the question—religion. It was a profound knowledge of the Aztecs that prompted Alfonso Caso to entitle his first version of *El pueblo del Sol,* "*La religión de los aztecas.*"

Religion touched the daily life of every man, woman, and child

[1] Bernal Díaz del Castillo, *Discovery and Conquest of Mexico* (New York, Farrar, Straus & Cudahy, 1956), 190–91.

in the Aztec world. It drove them to conquest and expansion, to build great temples, to compute and measure time, to offer hundreds of thousands in bloody sacrificial rites to their gods. It was, as Caso points out in this book, both the impetus and the nemesis of their civilization.

Today there are perhaps a million Aztec-Nahua–speaking residents of Mexico, the descendants of the great empire which Cortés and his lieutenants first saw 440 years ago. They and their ancestors have given many words and phrases not only to modern Spanish but to English as well. While Aztec art, architecture, engineering, astronomy, and perhaps even concepts of war were not original with these peoples, they came to be, as Alfred L. Kroeber said, the "administrators, legatees, dominators, and disseminators" of this culture. We are fortunate to be enabled to look deeply into the religion and way of life which lay behind all their achievements, as developed by one of the master scholars of aboriginal life in the Americas.

Lowell Dunham

Norman, Oklahoma

xvi

AUTHOR'S PREFACE

SEVERAL YEARS AGO, I published, under the title of *La religión de los aztecas,* a small book intended to acquaint the general public with a theme of fundamental importance for the understanding of the indigenous civilization that flourished in the central part of Mexico, a civilization that was swept away by the impact of the Spanish Conquest and colonization.

The object of the work was not, in general, to present new points of view, but simply to explain briefly the fundamental information and data that are available on the religion of the inhabitants of Tenochtitlán.

The Religion of the Aztecs was later translated into English (two printings were made of this version), and a popular edition in Spanish was issued by the Secretary of Public Education [Mexico] in a very fine collection entitled *Biblioteca Enciclopédica.*

All these editions are now out of print. Therefore, I thought it expedient to enlarge the original work considerably by using the greater knowledge that is now available on this subject and by taking advantage of the increasing interest of the public in acquiring more information about the indigenous cultures of the country. This, then, is not just another edition, but rather a new work, which makes use of the former one by enlarging and correcting it in certain parts. I have tried to retain the style of the first work and have attempted to point the account not toward specialists, but instead toward all who have an interest in the religion of a people who were fundamentally religious and whose worship of the gods was essential to their way of life. As I have said before, a knowledge of the religion of the Aztecs is indispensable to an understanding of the indigenous soul and is fundamental to an understanding of their reactions to nature and man in the intense drama of history.

I was fortunate in having an artist of the stature of the late Miguel Covarrubias to illustrate the book, an artist who also possessed a thorough knowledge of the ancient cultures of Mexico, and whose untimely death has removed a great student of Mexican antiquities and life.

Alfonso Caso

THE AZTECS

PEOPLE OF THE SUN

MAGIC AND RELIGION

MODERN MAN, accustomed to dealing with inanimate or animate nature with the resources derived from science and technology, finds it difficult to comprehend that other means of resolving, or trying to resolve, the problem of the control of the world have been employed. In a scientific civilization we are inclined to believe that in order to act upon natural forces we have no other course open than to know them first (this we call science), and to utilize them afterwards (this we call industry or technology), thereby deriving the norms of our action from the laws that we have discovered as generalizations of natural phenomena.

But it has not always been thus. Though man has always faced the same problems, he has often sought other solutions, nonscientific in character, which can be summed up in two great words having the respectability of things as old as humanity itself: *magic and religion*.

It has been said with great truth that fear and hope are the parents of the gods. Man, confronting nature, which frightens and overwhelms him, sensing his own inadequacy before forces that he neither understands nor is able to control but whose evil or propitious effects he suffers, projects his wonder, his fright, and his fear beyond himself, and since he can neither understand nor command, he fears and loves—in short, he worships.

Hence gods have been made in the image and likeness of man. Each human imperfection is transmuted into a god capable of overcoming it. Each human quality is projected into a divinity through which it acquires superhuman or ideal proportions.

But men have never been content merely to ask. Before laws were derived from the sciences, which now permit us to control some natural forces with relative precision, men of all lands and of all ages have thought that they had found in magic formulae the knowledge which would permit them to master their world. They have believed that natural forces are necessarily subject to words and acts of magic and that these forces must obey the conjuration of the one who pronounces the words or performs the acts.

3

From this point of view, magic and science are similar: both are procedures that have as their purpose the control of the world.

Whoever pronounces the magic spell is certain that nature will obey him, without regard to his intention, without even considering whether the incantation is pronounced for the purpose of achieving an objective or whether it is voiced inadvertently. We have only to recall the innumerable legends about the man who gets possession of the magic formula and, without realizing its potentialities, pronounces the words that set things in motion. A case in point is the sorcerer's apprentice who produced water but, since he did not know the formula to stop it, brought about a catastrophe. From this point of view, the magic formula acts independently, just as natural law operates independently, irrespective of the intent of the individual. If someone speaks the magic words or makes the magic gesture, the effect is produced, just as he who presses a button starts a machine, even though inadvertently, thereby producing the natural effect within modern technology. That is why there is a magic or natural necessity that operates objectively, without reference, in many cases, to the will of the individual.

Religion is quite different. In the first place, it requires the assistance of the will of the individual. A sin—that is to say, a transgression of the religious law—detaches itself little by little from the matrix of magic that envelops it, in order not to be considered as such, except when it is a voluntary infraction of a divine law.

There is, however, no religious necessity that binds the god to the prayer. The god cannot be forced to act by it, he is simply solicited to act in the way that the believer asks; but when the religious man confronts nature, which acts in its inexorable way, when he faces the magic formula or natural law, he knows that he has need of another will, the divine will, to which he can appeal in prayer.

Magic and religion differ from science in that they both admit, above and beyond the natural world of phenomena which our senses perceive or our intellect seizes upon, a supernatural world which surrounds and envelops this natural world. It is a magic or divine sphere where realities exist that are made manifest thereafter in the world of sense perception.

Science, on the other hand, continues on its way with a faith that phenomena will be repeated when the same circumstances exist, and that if man's senses are limited, his intelligence will enable him more and more to probe the depths of nature and control it for future ends.

Among some of the most primitive peoples, religious sentiment never develops into the form of a god with definite characteristics, that is, with personality. Natural forces are feared and worshiped, but a clear concept of a superhuman personality, one that disposes of the forces of nature at will and can harm or favor, is never developed.

On the other hand, all peoples who have achieved a certain level of cultural advancement personify their religious sentiments in their gods and conceive of them with human characteristics, though endowed with superhuman power. As a result of this conception, as Wundt points out,[1] the god always has certain characteristics of the hero. In this stage of cultural development, for each force, and sometimes for each aspect of natural force, there is created a personal god. This is polytheism.

Variation, change, and movement are explained as the struggle among the gods. Since the first thing that man perceives is the infinite variety of phenomena, he attributes this variety to a plurality of causes to which he assigns absolute free will and intelligence. The variation and the diversity of the world, the antagonism noted at times among the natural forces—trees uprooted by the hurricane or the coast lashed by the sea, the fire that consumes the forest or the earthquake that splits the earth asunder—are other manifestations of the struggle of the gods, of their passions and their caprices. But to the mind that perceives the apparent chaos in the world of phenomena there soon appears the philosophical necessity of seeking unity. Peoples with more advanced concepts of religion come to believe that everything in existence obeys the action of two antagonistic principles that struggle eternally. This is dualism. Only in this way can the struggle between good and evil be explained: there are placed in the good god all the qualities of strength, goodness, and beauty; and in the demon or evil god, to whom there is

[1] Wilhelm Wundt (1832–1920), a German physiologist, psychologist, and philosopher, born in Neckarau, Germany. His system of philosophy has been described as the science of the sciences. He attempted to unite in a consistent system the general knowledge contained in the various sciences.

5

also attributed great power, all evils and errors. Thus the world is conceived of as a struggle between the god and the devil, and one step further is taken toward the liberation of man the moment he thinks of himself as an active collaborator with the god in his struggle against the infernal powers. When this attitude reaches its peak, it will become evident, as it did to Plotinus, that the struggle between the good god and the evil god is not, after all, anything but the struggle between spirit and matter.

But man's need to philosophize does not allow him to stop here; he is able to conceive that even these two apparently antagonistic and contrary principles, evil and good, are reduced to a single principle, the cause and explanation of everything that exists. This is monism or monotheism.

Of course, we should be deceiving ourselves if we believed that these diverse aspects of religious sentiment occur in all people in the order indicated. We should be still more mistaken if we believed that an entire people changes suddenly from polytheism to dualism, and from the latter to monotheism. There are always certain individuals who, because of their superior intellect and development, are the first to abandon earlier beliefs and foresee the course that the religious culture of their people will take. Thus, in the sixth century before Christ, Xenophanes, anticipating the great philosophers of the Socratic era, was already saying that if oxen and horses had hands, they would fashion their gods in the images of oxen and horses. Of course, those religious and magical ideas that are the cultural heritage of many generations will not be abandoned by all individuals. Even in religions that have attained a monotheistic concept, some polytheistic rites and magical concepts and practices persist; and even in modern European culture, certain taboos, such as that regarding the number 13, exist, or practices inspired by polytheistic rites are continued.

Religion, like any other social phenomenon, does not become manifestly homogeneous until the entire culture of a people becomes homogeneous; but, when a people has lived in contact with other peoples and other cultures, the exceptional individuals are the first to perceive which practices are archaic and which decadent.

6

THE CHARACTER OF
THE AZTEC RELIGION

AT THE TIME of the Spanish Conquest, the religion of the Aztecs was polytheistic, based on the worship of a multitude of personal gods, most of them with well-defined attributes. Nevertheless, magic and the idea of certain impersonal and occult forces played an important role among the people. There was, in addition, among the uneducated classes, a tendency to exaggerate polytheism by conceiving of as gods, also, what, to the priests, were only manifestations or attributes of one god. Today, in a like manner, images of a saint are sometimes considered not only different but antagonistic, in spite of the fact that the Roman Catholic priest explains that the images are only two different aspects of the same saint.

But if there was a magic and impersonal background in the religion of the Aztec people, as well as an exaggerated polytheism, there is also evidence of the efforts of the Aztec priests to reduce the multiple divinities to different aspects of the same god, for when they adopted the gods of conquered peoples or received gods from peoples of more advanced culture, the priests always tried to incorporate them, as did the Romans, into their own national pantheon, by considering them as diverse manifestations of the gods they had inherited from the great civilizations which preceded them and from which they had derived their culture.

Thus it was, for example, that the god of wine was doubtless for the Mexican priests a single god, called Ometochtli because of his calendar name, which means "Two Rabbit." Nevertheless, in the manuscript known as the *Codex Magliabecchiano*,[1] we find a great many gods of pulque, with the characteristics of the region whence they came and names derived from those same areas. Thus we have the famous Tepoztécatl—or "he of the copper ax," who was the god of Tepoztlán, Morelos—as well as Toltécatl, the god of Tula, and Yautécatl, the god of Yautepec.

[1] A post-Columbian Mexican codex in the National Library, Florence, Italy.

7

While the Aztec priests tried to unite in a single concept the different gods of the different tribes and synthesize in a single power what were considered different gods, the people as a whole would not admit that their local god was subject to any other or that he was only an attribute of a superior being.

The only exceptions were Huitzilopochtli, the Aztecs' own tribal god, and the other deities associated with him in the national myths kept alive by Aztec pride. In legends of later times we see this god figuring among those who created the world, occupying a place similar to that held by the traditional Toltec and Teotihuacán gods and by those gods worshiped by the people of the Valley of Mexico before the volcano Xitle covered their homes with lava, several centuries before Christ.

However, as we shall see later, a very ancient school of philosophy held that the origin of all things was a single dual principle, masculine and feminine, that had created the gods, the world, and man. Certain exceptional men, like Nezahualcóyotl, the king of Texcoco, already preferred to worship an invisible god that could no longer be represented. He was called Tloque Nahuaque, or Ipalnemohuani, "the god of the immediate vicinity," "that one through whom all live," who was placed above the heavens and in the highest realm and on whom all things depended. If this is not a true monotheistic attitude because it still acknowledges the existence and the worship of other gods, it does indicate that in exceptional mentalities the philosophical desire for unity had already appeared and that men were seeking a single cause to explain all other causes, and a single god superior to all other gods, just as the gods were superior to all men.

Therefore, when Nezahualcóyotl built a temple in Texcoco upon a pyramid of nine terraces representing the nine heavens, he did not place in the sanctuary that crowned this pyramid any image representing the god, since "the one through whom all live" could not be portrayed and must be conceived as pure idea. Naturally this single god of Nezahualcóyotl did not have much following, nor did he affect the religious life of the people. The gods of philosophers have never been popular, for they arise from the need of a logical explanation of the universe, while the common people require less abstract gods who will satisfy their sentimental need for love and protection.

Tonacacíhuatl
(*Codex Telleriano-Remensis* 8).

THE CREATION OF THE GODS

We have already discussed a dual creative principle, masculine and feminine, from which the other gods originated by the process of generation. Their names indicate this duality: Ometecuhtli means "Two Lord," and Omecíhuatl, "Two Lady," and both resided in Omeyocan, "the place two." They were also called "the lord and lady of our flesh and sustenance" and were represented by symbols of fertility and adorned by ears of corn, for they were the origin of generation and the lord and mistress of food.

To be sure, these fundamental theogonic ideas were not an invention of the Aztecs. We have proof that the gods of generation were known in areas other than those conquered by the Aztecs. Thus, for example, in the *Codex Borgia*,[1] which comes without doubt from a region of Puebla

[1] A pre-Columbian codex now in the Ethnological Museum of the Vatican, Rome.

9

or Tlaxcala, we find these two gods mentioned as divinities propitious to generation and food.

Moreover, they appear associated with the first day of the ritual calendar, the Alligator, representative of the earth, as patrons of that day. This association indicates that they belong to a very old mythical tradition, since, as has been shown elsewhere, the ritual calendar existed in Mexico and Central America centuries before Christ.

This is not the only case which demonstrates that the Aztec religion was, in the vast majority of its concepts, a collection of ideas and practices derived from much older theogonic concepts and ritual practices. Indeed, some of these are so old that they are associated with the first appearance of sedentary cultures in Mesoamerica.

According to one of the versions that have come down thus, these two gods, Ometecuhtli and Omecíhuatl—also called Tonacatecuhtli and Tonacacíhuatl—had four sons to whom they entrusted the creation of the other gods, the world, and man. The four sons of the primitive divine pair were the Red Tezcatlipoca, also called Xipe and Camaxtle; the Black Tezcatlipoca, commonly called Tezcatlipoca; Quetzalcóatl, god of wind and of life; and Huitzilopochtli, the Blue Tezcatlipoca.

THE FOUR DIRECTIONS

ONE OF THE fundamental concepts of the Aztec religion was the grouping of all beings according to the four cardinal points of the compass and the central direction, or up and down. Therefore, in the Mexican mind the numbers 4 and 5 are very important, just as in Occidental magic the number 3 is significant.

The divine pair represented the central direction, or up and down, that is, the heaven and the earth, while their four sons were assigned to the four directions, or the four cardinal points of the compass. For that reason, three of them were characterized by different colors: red, black, and blue, corresponding to the East, the North, and the South, respectively, while Quetzalcóatl occupied the place that a white Tezcatlipoca, corresponding to the West, must have held in the primitive myth.

In fact, in the *Codex Bologna* or *Cospiano,*[1] there appears a white Tezcatlipoca with all the characteristics of the god of providence, from whom he differs only in color. The *Codex Bologna* belongs to the same Puebla-Tlaxcaltecan region as the *Codex Borgia,* mentioned in the previous section, and these manuscripts are painted in a style identical to that of the paintings which decorate the altars of Tizatlán in Tlaxcala, and of the polychrome ceramics that are found there and in many other sites in the Valley of Puebla, such as Tepeaca, Atlixco, and Totimihuacán. All of this demonstrates that the codices or pictorial manuscripts which have been correctly designated as the Borgia group belong to the cultures that flourished in the areas around Puebla and Tlaxcala.

This fundamental idea of the four cardinal points of the compass and the central direction, up and down, which made the fifth or central region, is found in all the religious manifestations of the Aztecs and is without doubt one of the concepts they inherited from the old cultures of Mesoamerica.

Not only were colors and gods grouped in this manner. Also animals, trees, days, and men, according to the day on which they were born, belonged to one of the four regions of the world. Man was given the name of the day of his birth within the ritual calendar of 260 days, which will be explained later. The calendar was divided into four parts of 65 days each, one part corresponding to the East, one to the North, one to the West, and one to the South, and these parts were repeated an infinite number of times.

[1] A pre-Columbian codex now in the library of the University of Bologna, Italy.

THE CREATION OF MAN

THE WORLD AND MAN have been created several times, according to the Aztecs, and each creation has been followed by a cataclysm that has destroyed mankind.

The last time man was created, according to one of the myths preserved by Mendieta,[1] Quetzalcóatl, the Mexican Prometheus, the beneficent god of all mankind, descended to the world of the dead to gather up the bones of past generations, and, sprinkling them with his own blood, created a new humanity.

Since man was created by the sacrifice of the gods, he must reciprocate by offering them his own blood in sacrifice. Human sacrifice was essential in Aztec religion, for if man could not exist except through the creative force of the gods, the latter in turn needed man to sustain them with human sacrifice. Man must nourish the gods with the magic sustenance of life itself, found in human blood and in the human heart.

MAN, THE COLLABORATOR OF THE GODS

THE IDEA that man is an indispensable collaborator of the gods, since the latter cannot subsist unless they are nourished, was clearly expressed in the sanguinary cult of Huitzilopochtli, a manifestation of the sun god.

Huitzilopochtli was the sun, the young warrior, born each morning from the womb of the old goddess of the earth and dying again each evening to illuminate with his dying light the world of the dead.

According to legend, Coatlicue, the old goddess of the earth, had become a priestess in the temple, living a life of retreat and chastity after

---

[1] Jerónimo de Mendieta (1525?–1604), a Franciscan friar, born in Vitoria, Spain. He came to Mexico in 1554, learned the native Indian languages, and became one of the great defenders of the Indians. He wrote his *Historia Eclesiástica Indiana* in 1596 or 1597; it was not published until 1870, in Mexico.

12

having given birth to the moon and the stars. One day while sweeping, she found a ball of down which she tucked away in her waistband. When she finished her tasks, she looked for the ball of feathers, but it had disappeared. Then she suddenly realized that she was pregnant. When her children, the moon, Coyolxauhqui, and the stars, called Centzonhuitznáhuac, discovered this, they became so furious that they determined to kill their mother.

Coatlicue wept over her approaching death as the moon and the stars armed to kill her, but the prodigy in her womb spoke to her and consoled her, saying that when the time came, he would defend her against all.

Just as her enemies came to slay the mother, Huitzilopochtli was born, and with the aid of the serpent of fire, the sun's ray, he cut off Coyolxauhqui's head and put the Centzonhuitznáhuac to flight.

So it was that when the god was born he had to open combat with his brothers, the stars, and his sister, the moon; and armed with the serpent of fire, he puts them to flight every day, his victory signifying a new day of life for men. When he consummates his victory, he is carried in a litter into the center of the sky by the spirits of warriors who have died in combat or on the sacrificial stone. When afternoon begins, he is picked up by the spirits of women who have died in childbirth, for they are equal to warriors because they, too, died taking a man prisoner—the newborn child. During the afternoon the souls of the mothers lead the sun to its setting, where the stars die and where the sun, like the eagle in his fall to death, is gathered close again by the earth. Each day this divine combat is begun anew, but in order for the sun to triumph, he must be strong and vigorous, for he has to fight against the unnumbered stars of the North and the South and frighten them all off with his arrows of light. For that reason man must give nourishment to the sun. Since the sun is a god, he disdains the coarse foods of mortals and can only be kept alive by life itself, by the magic substance that is found in the blood of man, the *chalchíhuatl,* "the precious liquid," the terrible nectar with which the gods are fed.

The Aztecs, the people of Huitzilopochtli, were the chosen people of the sun. They were charged with the duty of supplying him with food. For that reason war was a form of worship and a necessary activity that led them to establish the *Xochiyaóyotl,* or "flowery war." Its purpose, unlike that of wars of conquest, was not to gain new territories nor to exact tribute from conquered peoples, but rather to take prisoners for sacrifice to the sun. The Aztec was a man of the people chosen by the sun. He was the servant of the sun and consequently must be, above everything else, a warrior. He must prepare himself from birth for his most constant activity, the Sacred War, which was a kind of tournament in which the enemies "of the house," the Tlaxcaltecans, were the special challengers. They were the men who wore the lip plug curved in the form of a claw and, adorned like the Aztecs in their best finery, displayed great panaches of rich feathers and armor, and standards and shields sumptuously adorned with feather mosaic work and precious stones, copper plates, and golden bells.

THE CREATOR GODS

ACCORDING TO THE AZTECS, there were two gods who alternately created the various humanities that have existed: Quetzalcóatl, the beneficent god, the hero-founder of agriculture and industry; and the Black Tezcatlipoca, the all-powerful, multiform, and ubiquitous god, god of darkness, patron of sorcerers and evil ones. The struggle of these two gods is the history of the universe; their alternating victories so many other creations.

Traditions do not agree concerning the order of the different creations. According to one of them, the first epoch of the world, or the sun, began in this way:

The nocturnal Tezcatlipoca, whose *nahual* or disguise is the jaguar, its spotted skin resembling the heavens with their myriad stars, was the first to become a sun, and with him began the first era of the world. The first men created by the gods were giants; they neither sowed grain nor tilled the soil, but lived by eating acorns and other fruits and wild roots. Tezcatlipoca was also the constellation of Ursa Major, whom the Aztecs pictured as a jaguar. While he was ruling the world as the sun,

14

his enemy, Quetzalcóatl, struck him a blow with his staff. Tezcatlipoca fell into the water, changing into a jaguar. He devoured the giants, and the earth was depopulated and the universe was without a sun. This occurred on the day called "4 Jaguar."

Then Quetzalcóatl became the sun, until the jaguar struck him down with a blow of his paw. Then a great wind arose, and all the trees were uprooted, and the greater part of mankind perished. Those men who survived were transformed into monkeys, that is, into subhuman creatures. This took place on the day "4 Wind." Men at that time ate only pine nuts, or *acocentli*. The creator gods then chose Tláloc, the god of rain and celestial fire, as the sun, but Quetzalcóatl made fire rain down, and men either perished or were changed into birds. This happened on the day "4 Rain." The sustenance of men during this age was a seed called *acecentli*, or "water corn."

Then Quetzalcóatl selected Tláloc's sister as the sun. She was the goddess Chalchiuhtlicue, "the lady of the jade skirts," goddess of water. But no doubt it was Tezcatlipoca who caused it to rain so hard that the earth was flooded and men either perished or were transformed into fish. This occurred on the day called "4 Water." During this age men ate *cencocopi,* or *teocentli,* the ancestor of corn.

Since the sky, which is made of water, had fallen upon the earth, it was necessary for Tezcatlipoca and Quetzalcóatl to lift it up so that land might appear again. This is why, in the *Codex Vienna,*[1] Quetzalcóatl is holding up the sky with his hands.

According to other traditions, the first destruction was by a flood, and men were changed into fish; the second, by fire, and men were changed into birds; the third, by wind, and men were changed into monkeys; and the fourth and last, by jaguars, who devoured the giants, thereby leaving the world depopulated. In support of these traditions there is the fact that the giants, called *quinametzin,* are already mentioned in historical traditions as inhabiting the earth and fighting with men, principally in the region of Tlaxcala.

On the other hand, the destruction by water, fire, air, and jaguars and the conversion of human beings into fish, birds, monkeys, and

[1] The Codex Vienna is also known as the Codex Vindobonensis. A facsimile was published by Walter Lehmann and Ottokar Smital in 1929 in Vienna.

giants seem to point toward a concept, not of evolution, but rather of progression, in the various creation attempts made by the gods. This idea is also found, as we shall see, in the traditions of other peoples of Mesoamerica. Just as at the first attempt humanity would be transformed into fish and at the second into birds, the third effort would also fail, but men would now be changed into monkeys. At the fourth attempt they were already men, though barbarians, for they did not sow and they lived, as tradition says, by eating acorns and roots.

In the same way the different plants listed as the food of mankind continued progressively to approach the ideal foodstuff of the Mesoamerican, which, needless to say, is corn. Indeed, the last plant cited, the *cencocopi,* is none other than the *teocentli,* a plant similar to corn, which is generally considered to be the wild ancestor of this grass, or rather, according to the latest investigations, one of the plants which through hybridization produced present-day corn. At times only the esoteric names of the different foods of past humanities are given; thus acorns are called "7 Grass"; the *acocentli,* "12 Serpent"; the *acecentli* (milium), "4 Flower"; and the *teocentli,* "7 Flint"; while modern corn is called "7 Serpent."

There was in the concept of multiple creations, in addition to the feeling of a divine effort which the gods destroy as imperfect, the idea that the worlds that were continually being created were gradually nearing perfection.

For the Aztecs, therefore, not all past ages were the best. The golden age must not be placed at the beginning of the world, for the gods, in their continuing efforts with multiple creations, finally succeeded in finding the formula which led to the creation of a perfect humanity and a perfect foodstuff.

This idea of multiple creations agrees largely with the myths that have come down to us from the Quichés, for in their sacred book, the *Popol Vuh,*[2] it is related that the creator made several attempts before he achieved a perfect result. Thus the deer and the birds were created

[2] *Popol Vuh, Popo Vuh,* or *Popol Buh,* literally the "Book of the Community." See *Popol Vuh: The Sacred Book of the Ancient Quiché Maya,* English version by Delia Goetz and Sylvanus G. Morley from the translation of Adrián Recinos (Norman, University of Oklahoma Press, 1950).

16

first, but since they could not lift their voices in prayer to heaven, they were condemned, and "their flesh shall be ground between the teeth." The second creation was clay men and the third, wooden men, but they had to be destroyed because they had no hearts and could not praise the gods. Only when the gods used corn seed to make the body of man could he have life, and the four men made with corn were able at last to utter words of thanks to the gods for their creation.

We also find here the idea that the gods demanded constant worship from men, and that creation was not a gracious gift to man from the gods but rather in the nature of a contract carrying an obligation for man to worship the gods continually.

Moreover, according to *Popol Vuh,* the Quiché myth, like the Aztec myth, indicates the belief that the barbarians who did not plant corn or have the organized cults of the great Central American theocracies were like poor imitations of men, that must be destroyed because the dawn of culture had not appeared to them. Further, the idea of multiple creations was, as among the Aztecs, the expression of progressive attempts made by the gods, in first creating animals and afterwards trying better and better materials until they struck upon corn, here again the divine substance of which the body of man is formed.

When the last humanity of the several created previously was destroyed, whether by flood, as one of the traditions has it, or whether because the gods killed the giants, as another relates, the sun was also lost in the catastrophe, and there was no one left to light the world. Then all the gods gathered in Teotihuacán and decided that one of them should be sacrificed and changed into the sun.

Two of the gods volunteered for the sacrifice. One, rich and powerful, prepared himself by offering balls of copal and liquidambar to the father of the gods, but instead of maguey spines stained with his own blood, he offered spines made of precious coral. The other god, poor and sick, could offer only balls of grass and maguey spines dyed in the blood of his own sacrifice.

For four consecutive days the gods who were to undergo the trial fasted and sacrificed. On the fifth day, all the deities arranged themselves in two rows, at the end of which was placed the sacred brazier in which a great fire burned. The chosen gods must hurl themselves into the flames so that they might emerge purified to illuminate the world with their brilliance.

The poor god and the rich god made ready for the trial. It fell to the lot of the rich god to make the first attempt, since he was the more powerful. Three times he lunged forward, only to stop at the edge of the great fire each time, not daring to take the final leap.

The destitute god then tried his valor. Closing his eyes, he leaped into the middle of the divine brazier, which sent forth a great tongue of flame. When it died down, the rich god, shamed by his cowardice, hurled himself into the fire, and he, too, was consumed. The jaguar also leaped into the ashes, and he came out with his coat spotted; and the eagle also threw himself in, and that is why his tail-feathers and wings are black.

The sacrificed gods had vanished, but still there was no sun. The other deities were troubled, wondering where it would appear. At last, out came the sun, and almost immediately thereafter the moon burst forth, shining as brightly as the sun! Enraged by the audacity of the moon, the gods struck it in the face with a rabbit, leaving a mark which it carries to this day. Thus did the Aztecs explain the spots on the moon as representing the figure of a rabbit.

But the sun did not move. It hung on the horizon and seemed reluctant to start on its journey. The other gods sought the reason, and terrible was the reply. The sun demanded that the other gods, the stars, be offered in sacrifice. One of them, the planet Venus, shot an arrow at the sun to wound him, but the sun seized it and with that same arrow shot her dead; and one by one the other gods died at the hands of the sun. The twin brother of Venus, Xólotl, was the last to die. It is he who is sometimes the first and sometimes the last star to disappear among the rays of the rising sun. Since Xólotl, in addition to being the god of twins and of monsters, was also a very clever sorcerer, his death was not easy to accomplish. He changed himself first into double maguey, called *mexólotl,* and then into double corn, then into many other double things or monstrosities, and finally, into the *axólotl,* or *"ajolote"* (the salamander), which lives in water, and it was there that the sun killed him.

In the Aztec myth of the creation of the suns there is a facet which we do not find in the Quiché book; namely, the belief that this fifth

Quetzalcóatl *(Codex Borbonicus* 22).

sun, which currently gives us light, was also to die as the others died, and his end would be brought about by earthquakes on a day called "4 Earthquake."

This catastrophe was expected to take place precisely on the last day of an Aztec century, a cycle of fifty-two years. At nightfall on this day all the fires in the city were put out, and the priests led the people in solemn procession to a temple atop the Hill of the Star, near Ixtapalapa. There they waited until midnight, and if the star they were observing, undoubtedly Aldebaran, either in conjunction with the Pleiades or the Ram, passed in his course over what they considered the middle of the sky, it meant that the world would not come to an end and that the sun would rise the following day to renew his struggle with the powers of night. But if Aldebaran, called Yohualtecuhtli, had not followed its course on that night, then the stars and the planets, the *tzitzimime,* changed into fearful beasts, must return to earth, to devour man before the earthquakes destroyed the sun.

Thus when Aldebaran passed the meridian, fire was kindled and carried joyfully to the local temples and thence to the homes of the people, as an indication that the gods had taken pity on mankind and were granting men another century of life.

It should be noted that the end of each epoch, in the legend of the suns, fell on a day that carried the numeral 4. The same circumstance occurred among the Mayas, for in their count the age just prior to the present one ended on a day with the name "4 Ahau," as likewise had the age preceding it.

Xólotl (*Codex Borgia* 10).

THE RAIMENT OF THE GODS

IN BEGINNING the study of the complicated Aztec pantheon, one must take into consideration the fact that the various gods, in sculpture and in the paintings in the manuscripts, are always identified by specific articles of clothing, and sometimes by the objects they carry in their hands. One rarely finds representations of the gods with their hieroglyphic names, which are the same as the days of their birth. As a rule, it is necessary to analyze the many details of a god's attire in order to identify him.

The bearded Quetzalcóatl
(*Codex Magliabecchiano* 61).

Sometimes it is quite difficult to be certain of the identity of a god, especially if there is no coloring, as is the case with most pieces of sculpture, for the same ornament, in different colors, may be characteristic of two different gods. For example, a kind of pleated paper fan worn on the back of the neck is a characteristic of the water gods, the gods of the mountains, and the gods of vegetation. This fan is white for the goddess Iztaccíhuatl, the snow-capped mountain; red for Chicomecóatl, goddess of corn; blue for Chalchiuhtlicue, goddess of water; and green for Tepeyolohtli, god of the mountains.

A description of Quetzalcóatl as he appears in a painting in the *Codex Borbonicus*[1] will furnish an excellent example of the complicated attire of the gods.

The body and face of the god are painted black, since he was the pre-eminent priest and the originator of the self-sacrifice which con-

[1] A pre-Columbian codex now in the library of the Chamber of Deputies, Paris.

sisted of drawing blood from the ears and other parts of the body by pricking them with maguey spines and eagle or jaguar bone needles. Hence we see a bone in his headdress, from which hangs a green band terminating in a blue disk—the symbol of the *chalchíhuatl,* "the precious liquid," human blood. As further sacerdotal attributes, he carries in one hand an incense pot with a handle in the form of a serpent and in the other a bag for copal.

Covering his mouth there is a red mask in the form of a bird's beak, which in some representations is also set with the fangs of a serpent. This mask identifies him as the god of wind, in which form he was worshiped under the name of Ehécatl, meaning "wind."

The dead Sun *(Codex Borgia* 30).

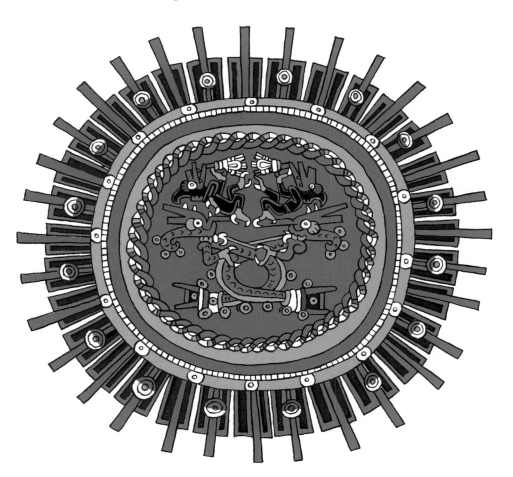

On his head he wears a conical cap made of ocelot skin, called *ocelocopilli;* it is tipped with a turquoise ornament and held in place by a tuft made of loops. The breastpiece edged with shells, the bracelets, and the ankle bands are likewise made of ocelot skin. His breastplate, called *ehecailacacózcatl,* or "breastplate of the wind," is formed by the transverse cut of a large sea shell, and his earplug is a turquoise disk from which hangs a red tassel and an object of twisted shell called *epcololli,* "twisted shell."

On the back of the neck he wears a panache made from the black feathers of the crow and the large red feathers of the macaw. This ornament, which appears in a painting in the *Codex Borgia,* symbolizes the sun at night, that is, the dead sun.

In other paintings, Quetzalcóatl generally wears a beard, not because he was a European, as was previously believed, but because as a creator god he was portrayed as an old man and consequently bearded, just as the gods of antiquity are portrayed, especially the most primitive gods.

COMPLEXITY OF
THE AZTEC PANTHEON

ONE OF the greatest difficulties encountered in any attempt to understand Aztec mythology is the multiplicity of gods and the diversity of attributes of the same god. This is due, as has been said, to the fact that Aztec religion was in a period of synthesis, in which there were being grouped together, within the concept of a single god, different capacities that were considered to be related. Quetzalcóatl, one of the greatest of the gods, provides an example of how different and seemingly unrelated aspects were being synthesized in a single god. He was Quetzalcóatl, the god of wind, of life, and of the morning; the planet Venus, god of twins and of monsters; and so on. According to these diverse

23

attributes, he was known by various names: Ehécatl, Quetzalcóatl, Tlahuizcalpantecuhtli, Ce Ácatl, Xólotl, etc.

The name Quetzalcóatl means literally "quetzal-serpent" or "the plumed serpent," but since to the Mexican the feathers of the quetzal bird were a symbol of something precious and cóatl also means "twin brother," the name Quetzal-cóatl may also be translated esoterically as "the precious twin," thereby indicating that the morning and the evening star are one and the same, that is, the planet Venus, represented in the morning by Quetzalcóatl and in the afternoon by his twin brother, Xólotl. Therefore, Tlahuizcalpantecuhtli appears with two faces, one of a living man, the other in the form of a skull.

This identification of the morning and evening stars has given rise to many myths among mankind and explains almost all the legends associated with Quetzalcóatl.

In reality, Venus does appear for some time as an evening star, then it disappears, and when it reappears, is a morning star. The myth explains this astronomical phenomenon by relating that Quetzalcóatl and his twin brother, Xólotl, descended to the world of the dead and, wandering in hell, underwent various trials imposed by the infernal gods.

According to the myth, Quetzalcóatl decided to ask the god of the underworld for the bones of dead men with which to create a new man, and the twin brothers set out on their journey. When they arrived in the underworld, they made their plea before Mictlantecuhtli, begging him for the bones, but since Quetzalcóatl knew, as the chronicler says, that the god of the dead was "double-dealing and mistrustful," he began to run as soon as he got them. Mictlantecuhtli, angered by his escape, pursued him and ordered the quail to attack him. Quetzalcóatl slipped during his flight, was attacked by the birds, fell, broke the bones, and scarcely had time to pick up the fragments and escape with them from the underworld. The two brothers conferred, and, in spite of the fact that the affair did not turn out as well as they had hoped, Quetzalcóatl offered a sacrifice over the bones. Sprinkling them with his own blood, he created a new race of men. But as the bone fragments were of different sizes, so too are the men and women in the world; and the quail, as a result of their daring pursuit of the god, were to be sacrificed and their blood sprinkled on the sacrificial altars, for they were the collaborators of the god of the underworld and had attempted to prevent the hero from carrying out his mission.

Men are, then, the children of Quetzalcóatl, and the god always appears in this benevolent guise, as their father and creator.

The myth of the twin brothers spread beyond the borders of Mexico and Central America and is frequently found among other American peoples.

Likewise, the flight of Quetzalcóatl from Tula to the mythical Tlillan Tlapallan, "the land of the black and the red," and his promise to return from the East in the year of his name, *Ce Ácatl,* is but a mythical explanation of the death of the planet, his descent into the West, where the black and the red, night and day, merge, and the prophecy that he will reappear in the East as the morning star, preceding the sun.

Therefore, when the conquistadors landed at Veracruz, in the year 1519, called *Ce Ácatl* ("One Reed") in the Aztec calendar, Montezuma was sure that here was Quetzalcóatl, returning to take possession of his Toltec kingdom, which he had abandoned when he fled to Tlillan Tlapallan.

As the god of life, Quetzalcóatl appears as the constant benefactor of mankind, and so we find that after having created man with his own blood, he sought a way to nourish him. He discovered corn, hidden by the ants within a hill, and changing himself into an ant, stole a grain, which he later gave to man. He taught man how to polish jade and other precious stones and how to locate deposits of them. He showed him how to weave multicolored fabrics from the miraculous cotton that grew in different colors; he taught him how to do mosaic work with the feathers of the quetzal bird, the bluebird, the hummingbird, the macaw, and other birds with brilliant plumage. But above all he taught man science, thereby endowing him with the means to measure time and study the movements of the stars; he taught him how to arrange the calendar and devised ceremonies and fixed certain days for prayers and sacrifices.

Quetzalcóatl is a very ancient god. Among the Mayas and the Quichés he was known as Kukulkán and Gucumatz; and even though we do not know his name, he appears as the feathered serpent in the most ancient of the Teotihuacán ruins, predating the Toltec era. A Zapotec god is frequently pictured on the clay pots peculiar to this culture and its predecessors in the Valley of Oaxaca. This god has so many characteristics similar to those of Quetzalcóatl that he appears to be a representation of him.

The multiplicity of Quetzalcóatl's functions also indicates the great antiquity of his cult and the veneration in which he was held in all Mesoamerica. Perhaps the most important aspect of this god, still little known, is his relation to the concepts of holiness and sin. In the Toltec era, his struggle with his brother, Tezcatlipoca, assumes characteristics that are not only mythical but also historical.

In short, Quetzalcóatl is the very essence of saintliness; his life of fasting and penitence, his priestly character, and his benevolence toward his children, mankind, are evident in the material that has been preserved for us in the chronicles and in the picture-writing of the indigenous manuscripts. But side by side with this aspect of saintliness we find also in Quetzalcóatl an aspect of sin; and sin, to the indigenes, meant drunkenness and failure to observe sexual abstinence.

The sinner is pictured in the codices as the "eater of filth." Sin was just that, a moral filth, and it assumed tragic proportions when Quetzalcóatl, the very archtype of saintliness, allowed himself to be dragged into drunkenness and incontinence. To be sure, he was led astray by Tezcatlipoca, the god of evil, and, as has been said, in the long-drawn-out struggle that these two rival gods carried on, creating and destroying the universe only to create and destroy it again, Tezcatlipoca, the evil one, finally used seduction as a means of making the holy Quetzalcóatl fall into sin. In like manner, according to another myth, the goddess of love and beauty, Xochiquetzal, seduced the virtuous Yappan, provoking the wrath of the gods, who changed him into a scorpion.

In this way the cosmic struggle was changed into a moral struggle, and later, when the Toltec king, the historical Quetzalcóatl, was forced to leave Tula, the priests and the faithful followers of Tezcatlipoca pursued him and forced him to abandon the central region of Mexico and flee to the lands of Veracruz, Tabasco, and Yucatán.

The hypothesis that Quetzalcóatl may have been an importation of European ideas to American soil should be completely discarded. Long before the American continent was discovered—that is, long before the European could have undertaken expeditions to the American continent, even before the Christian era—Quetzalcóatl was already in existence. The association of the white, long-bearded god of the legend with an Irish bishop or with the apostle St. Thomas is only one of many such errors that by dint of repetition acquire the dignity of truth. Quetzalcóatl, the bearded god, is a very ancient god of Mesoamerica. Even before the Christian era his cult was in existence in this region of the world. He is by no means a god foreign to Mexico; he is, on the contrary, one of the most important and characteristic gods of that part of the world.

TEZCATLIPOCA

ANOTHER OF THE most important gods, and perhaps the one who has the most diverse forms, is the creator god, Tezcatlipoca. Originally he symbolized the night sky, and for that reason he is related to the stellar gods, to the moon, and to those that signify death, evil, or destruction. He was the patron of sorcerers and of highwaymen, but at the same time he was the eternally young, the Telpochtli, "he who never grows old," and Yáotl, "the enemy," the patron of warriors, and hence was associated with Huitzilopochtli.

His name means "the mirror that smokes," because, as Pomar says,[1] his im-

[1] Juan Bautista Pomar, a Mexican writer of the sixteenth century born in Texcoco. He was a mestizo, the son of a Spaniard and the grandson of the King of Nezahualpitzintli. In 1582 he wrote *Relación de Texcoco*. It was published in the nineteenth century by García de Icazbalceta, Mexico.

Técpatl (*Codex Borbonicus* 20).

age was painted with soot containing shining metallic flecks which the Indians called *tezcapoctli,* or "shining smoke."

Tezcatlipoca was primarily the god of providence; he was omnipresent and omniscient in all human affairs. Consequently, directly or under one of his many names, he was worshiped not only in Tenochtitlán but also in many other parts of Mexico, and especially in Texcoco.

In some ways he was akin to Huitzilopochtli, and in others he was his opposite; for Huitzilopochtli represented the blue sky, the sky of day, while Tezcatlipoca personified the black or night sky. He was the warrior of the North, while Huitzilopochtli was the warrior of the South.

He was also the discoverer of fire, even though this element had as its special patron the god Xiuhtecuhtli, the lord of the year, also called Huehuetéotl, the "old god," and Ixcozauhqui, "yellow face."

Tezcatlipoca was the patron of princes, and he himself was called

Tezcatlipoca (*Codex Borgia* 17—a reconstruction).

28

Nezahualpilli, "the prince who fasts," and under the calendar name of *Ome Ácatl,* he presided over feasts and banquets.

His fetish was the flint or obsidian knife, and so he was called Técpatl or Iztli; he was the lord of cold and ice, with the name of Iztlacoliuhqui, "the curved flint knife"; he was also the god of sin and misery. The jaguar, Tepeyolohtli, "the heart of the mount," was his disguise.

He presided over the homes of both young warriors and bachelors, over *Tel-*

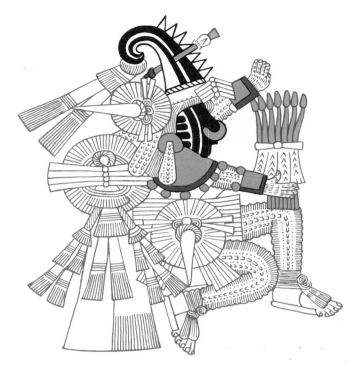

Iztlacoliuhqui (*Codex Borbonicus* 12).

pochcalli, the popular school of war attended by the young plebians, while Quetzalcóatl was the patron of the *Calmécac,* the school for the nobles, from whom the high chiefs of the army, the priests, and the judges and the kings were chosen.

Since he was young, he was the first to arrive at the festivities when the gods returned, in the month of *Teotleco.* He carried off old Tláloc's wife, Xochiquetzal, goddess of flowers and love, of whom he said:

> I believe that she is truly a goddess, that she is really very beautiful and fine. I shall have her, not tomorrow nor the next day nor the next, but right now, at this moment, for I, in person, am he who ordains and commands it so. I am the young warrior who shines like the sun and has the beauty of the dawn.

Tezcatlipoca can be identified in the codices by the smoking mirror that he wears at his temple and by another which he wears in place of the foot torn off by the earth monster, as recounted in a myth explaining

29

Tezcatlipoca and Huitzilopochtli (the *cuauhxicalli* of the jaguar; *cuauhxicalli,* literally, "eagle vase"—stone boxes or containers generally made of lava elaborately decorated inside and out and used for burning and storing human hearts).

why at times in more southern latitudes one of the stars of the constellation Ursa Major disappears from the heavens, below the horizon.

Being a nocturnal god, Tezcatlipoca was also painted black, but his face was striped with yellow and black horizontal bars. This decoration, known by the name of *ixtlán tlatlaan,* characterizes all the Tezcatlipocas, but in Xipe the colors change to red and yellow, and in Huitzilopochtli to blue and yellow.

30

Tezcatlipoca's hair is cut in two different lengths, a style called *tzotzocolli,* characteristic of warriors; and the god carries the *aztaxelli,* an ornament of heron feathers; the shield, the *chimalli;* the dart hurler, *átlatl;* and the darts, *tlacochtli*—all of which mark him as a warrior.

Since the Aztecs considered the North the homeland of the hunting tribes to whom they gave the generic name of Chichimecs, the god of the Chichimecs, Mixcóatl, god of the hunt, was also related to Tezcatlipoca.

What has been said of this god shows the intricate relationships that existed among the Aztec deities and demonstrates that only by a minute analysis of their attributes and the myths about them can we hope to understand the nature of the gods and the mysteries of their cults.

Tepeyolohtli
(*Codex Borbonicus* 3).

THE WORSHIP OF THE SUN, THE MOON, AND THE STARS

WE HAVE already seen that the Aztecs tried to explain celestial phenomena through myths that recount the struggle of the gods—that is, the struggle of the heavenly bodies. This led them to make exact observations, which they recorded on their monuments and in their codices, that are evidence of the advanced stage they had reached in the science of astronomy. It also led them to adopt a calendar, which was undoubt-

31

The four Suns (center of the Aztec calendar).

edly the product of the older cultures that had preceded them. Even though it is inferior to the admirable computation made by the Mayas, which is still not surpassed by our present-day system, the Aztec calendar has, none the less, elements that make it an extraordinary scientific development for a people who were, in other fields, very far from the cultural level it indicated.

The sun, called Tonatiuh, was invoked by the names of "the shining one," "the beautiful child," "the eagle that soars." He was generally represented by a disk, decorated in Aztec fashion. This disk is widely known because it is an essential part of the celebrated monument called the Aztec Calendar, which is simply a very elaborate representation of the sun.

In the center of the disk is the face of Tonatiuh; at the sides appear his hands, tipped with eagle claws clutching human hearts, for the sun was looked upon by the Aztecs as an eagle. In the morning, as he rose into the sky, he was called Cuauhtlehuánitl, "the eagle who ascends"; in the evening he was called Cuauhtémoc, "the eagle who fell," the name of the last, unfortunate, heroic Aztec emperor.

Around the figure of Tonatiuh there are sculptured in large dimensions the date "4 Earthquake," the day on which the present sun is to be destroyed by earthquakes. In the rectangles of the sign "earthquake" are the dates on which the former suns perished ("4 Jaguar"; "4 Wind," represented by the head of the god Ehécatl-Quetzalcóatl; "4 Rain," represented by the head of Tláloc; "4 Water," represented by a jar of water from which emerges the bust of the goddess Chalchiuhtlicue).

A ring surrounding these figures contains other representations of the signs of the days. Beginning at the top with the head of the alligator *Cipactli,* the ring closes with the sign for the flower, *Xóchitl.* Then follow the bands with drawings of the solar rays and of jewels of jade or turquoise, for the Aztecs called the sun *Xiuhpiltontli,* "the turquoise child." They thought of him as the most precious thing in the universe and always pictured him as a jewel. Finally, the two outer bands are the two fire serpents who bear the sun through the sky. Between their fangs appear the faces of the deities who use these serpents as disguises.

These serpents of fire, or *xiuhcóatls,* that surround the sun also circled the Great Temple of Tenochtitlán and formed the famous *coatepantli,* or "wall of serpents." Nothing of the latter remains today except a few heads, which are in the National Museum of Mexico. In another temple at Tenayuca, however, such heads can be seen surrounding the temple dedicated to the sun.

Huitzilopochtli fittingly represents the blue sky, or the sky of day, but he is an incarnation of the sun. His struggle with the nocturnal powers led by the moon has already been recounted, and how he must defeat the gods of night each day in order to keep mankind alive and prevent the gods of darkness from destroying the sun. It has also been

33

Moon with rabbit; moon with flint knife (*Codex Borgia* 55, 50).

pointed out that Huitzilopochtli, unlike the majority of the other gods, seems to have occupied a place of importance only among the Aztecs. Indeed, up to the present time, the only representation of this god in any manuscript that comes from a region outside the Tenochtitlán area that has been brought to our attention is the one pointed out by Beyer[1] in the Fejérvary-Mayer manuscript,[2] though the same Mexican god appears to be portrayed in a painting adorning the temples of Tulum, a Mayan city that came under strong Toltec influence.

However, the tribal character of Huitzilopochtli is clearly revealed in the legends of the Aztec migrations preserved in the codices and chronicles and in the foundations of Tenochtitlán.

As a matter of fact, it was Huitzilopochtli who, in the year "One Flint," the year of his birth, induced the leaders of the Aztec tribe to leave their mythical homeland, Aztlán, located in the middle of a lake, and undertake the long wanderings before establishing themselves on another island, also located in the middle of a lake, which would have

[1] The late Hermann Beyer, a German scientist, formerly associated with the Middle American Research Institute at Tulane University. He was an authority on Mayan hieroglyphics and Middle American archaeology.

[2] The Codex Fejérvary-Mayer, an old Mexican picture manuscript now in the Liverpool, England, Free Public Museum.

Huitzilopochtli (*Codex Borbonicus* 34).

not only the same physical but also the same mythical conditions as the place from which they had come. During their wanderings Huitzilopochtli was careful to arrange what his people should do; and his spokesmen, who carried his statue, whence came their name, *teomama,* told the people when they must settle and when they must abandon the places where they had taken up their abode. In this way they spent centuries wandering through the north and central parts of Mexico until they finally settled down in the valley.

Since the god had promised to give his people a definite homeland

35

and dominion over the world, it was necessary for the Aztecs to remain separate from the other indigenous nations, their enemies. This was so necessary that when they were firmly established in the valley and commercial relations and marriages began to break their isolation, the priests were careful to see that a king's daughter who had been given in marriage to an Aztec prince was sacrificed. Hostilities would then break out again, and long-smoldering hatreds would be stirred between the Aztecs and the tribes they were destined to conquer.

But after they left the land of whiteness, they had to establish themselves in a place that was to be revealed by magical manifestations. When the astonished priests found the eagle poised on the cactus, the omen Huitzilopochtli had given them, the trees turned white and the waters became white; there the Aztecs were to found Tenochtitlán. A stream of blue water and another of red gushed forth from the spring, indicating the hieroglyphic *atltlachinolli,* which means "water, a burned thing," or the holy war which had as its objective the offering of the blood and hearts of the victims to the sun.

Metzli, the moon, is also pictured at times with a disk decorated on its outer bands like the solar disk, but generally this disk is black or ash-colored. At the center there appears the figure of a bone twisted into a form resembling a cross section of a small jar of water or the figure of a rabbit, as explained in the legend about the sun, the moon, and the rabbit.

The eagle and the jaguar were the creatures in which

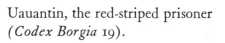

Uauantin, the red-striped prisoner (*Codex Borgia* 19).

the powers of light and darkness were incarnate. Warriors who attained the great honor of being called by these names were more dedicated than others to supplying nourishment to the sun by sacrifice.

The astral gods, being victims of the sun, appear in the codices with their bodies painted with white chalk, striped in red, just as the Aztecs painted the prisoners of war who were to be sacrificed. Facial painting in the form of a black mask marks them as gods of the night.

There were many astral deities, but the most important were Mixcóatl, "the cloud serpent," or the Milky Way; Camaxtle, tutelar god of the Tlaxcaltecans; Tlahuizcalpantecuhtli, "the lord of the house of dawn," etc. All the stars, conceived of as gods, were thought to be grouped in two squadrons called *Centzon Mimixcoa*, "the unnumbered ones from the North," and *Centzon Huitznáhuac*, "the unnumbered ones from the South." They were the warriors against whom the sun must do battle each day.

But the planets were the *tzitzimime*, or *tzontémoc*, "those who fell head first," that is, those who seemed to fall into the west, distinguishing thereby their course of movement from that of the other stars. It is they who, transformed into jaguars on the terrible night at the end of the century, will come down to earth, changed into wild beasts, to devour man.

Tlahuizcalpantecuhtli and Mixcóatl *(Codex Borgia* 19, 25).

37

THE GODS OF FIRE

LIKE WATER, air, and earth, fire also had its special god. His name indicates the great antiquity of his cult, for the Aztecs called him Huehuetéotl, which means "the old god," and he was always pictured as an old man.

In contrast to the young Tezcatlipoca, who was the first to arrive at the feast of the month of *Teotleco,* Huehuetéotl was the last to appear at the reunion of the gods.

The old Teotihuacán culture, which flourished during the first centuries of the Christian era, represented him as an old man burdened with age and bearing on his head an enormous brazier. His stooped back, his toothless mouth, and the wrinkles at the corners of his lips give him his characteristic appearance of decrepitude.

But the god of fire appears not only in Teotihuacán but also in other contemporary cultures and even in older ones. Indeed, this god appears on a brazier found at the Olmec site of the hill of Las Mesas and on Zapotec urns. What is perhaps the oldest figure of him that has been discovered was found in an archaeological site in the Valley of Mexico where the Ticomán culture was in full flower when the volcano Xitle erupted, several centuries before the Christian era.

The god of fire undoubtedly represents one of the oldest conceptions of Mesoamerican man. He was the god of the center position in relation to the four cardinal points of the compass, just as the *tlecuil,* or brazier for kindling fire, was the center of the indigenous home and temple. For this reason, the figure of the cross is frequently found on the priests of the god, just as it is also found adorning the great incense pots called *tlemaitl*—literally "hands of fire"—in which the priests burned incense to the gods. To be sure, a god as old as this one also had many attributes. He was called Xiuhtecuhtli, which means "the lord of the year," "the lord of grass," or "the lord of turquoise," since the word *xiúhuitl,* with a slight variation in intonation, means all three things. He is frequently pictured carrying a kind of blue mitre made of turquoise mosaic work, which distinguished the Mexican kings and was called *xiuhuitzolli*. His *nahual,* or disguise, was the Xiuhcóatl, or the serpent of fire. It is characterized, as has been said, by a kind of horn decorated with the figures of seven stars and worn over the nose.

In the discussion of the stone called the Aztec Calendar the two serpents, or fire dragons, were mentioned that transport the sun on his course through the sky; and on two sides of the pyramid of Tenayuca, a temple dedicated to the worship of the sun, there are serpents of fire painted black or blue to indicate the two dragons, from the North and from the South, which carry the sun on his path.

Thus the nocturnal Tezcatlipoca and the diurnal Huitzilopochtli, were also gods of fire, and occasionally donned Xiuhcóatl, the *nahual* peculiar to Xiuhtecuhtli.

Many ceremonies and sacrifices were dedicated to this god, and at one of the cruelest ceremonies men were burned in his honor.

But Xiuhtecuhtli as god of the year was also of great importance. During one of the most elaborate festivals, celebrated every eight years, when the 584-day period of the planet Venus and the years of the sun form a cycle, a great ceremony was held in honor of Xiuhtecuhtli, and the first month of the year, *Izcalli,* was dedicated to the worship of this particular god.

According to legend, a man and woman discovered fire, and when they had done so, they began to roast fish to eat, but the gods, angered at the boldness of the discovery made without their consent, cut off their heads and changed them into dogs.

In Mexican mythology, as in Greek mythology, the bold man capable of getting possession of fire, symbol of human power, without the consent of the gods, must be punished; he pays with his life for having the audacity to think that men are sufficient unto themselves to solve their problems.

Tláloc (*Codex Magliabecchiano* 32).

THE GODS OF WATER
AND OF VEGETATION

FOR A PEOPLE essentially agricultural, as were the Aztecs, the rainy season and other atmospheric phenomena that influenced their crops were of fundamental importance. Thus it is not surprising that the worship of the gods of water and of vegetation should occupy a great part of their religious life.

Tláloc, "he who makes things grow," god of the rains and of lightning, is the most important deity in this group of gods. He is also very probably the most ancient of the gods worshiped by man in Mexico and Central America.

The Mayas called him Chac, the Totonacs called him Tajín, the Mixtecs worshiped him under the name of Cocijo. In all parts of Mexico and Central America, worship of him is so old that its beginnings are lost in the remoteness of antiquity.

He was the principal god of the Olmec culture and appears with the mask of the jaguar-serpent on the colossal axes and the clay and jade figurines of this very ancient and advanced culture.

In Teotihuacán representations of him outnumber those of Quetzalcóatl, and his important cult very likely extended as far as the tribes that encircled the region of the high Mesoamerican cultures to the north and the south.

He is not a creator god, however; rather, he was created, like the other gods, by the children of the divine pair. The legend reads as follows:

In order to create the god and goddess of water, all four gods gathered together and made Tlalocatecuhtli and his wife Chalchiuhtlicue, god and goddess of water, and from them one sought water when it was needed. It is said that the abode of the god of water has four rooms, and that in the middle of a large patio there are four large jars of water. The water in one jar is very good, and from this jar come the rains when grain and seeds sprout and the weather is good. In another jar the water is bad, and when the rains come from this jar, cobwebs form on the grain and the grain mildews. The third jar contains water that sends freezing rains; the fourth jar sends the rains that prevent the grain from heading or cause it to wither. And this god of water, in order to send rain, created many priests with small bodies, and they live in the four rooms of the rain god's house and they hold small containers in one hand in which they draw the water from those jars, and in the other hand they hold sticks, and when the rain god commands them to go and take the rains to certain areas, they take their pots and their sticks and they pour forth the water that was ordered of them, and when it thunders, that is when they break their containers with the sticks, and when the lightning flashes, that is because of what they had in the pots or a part of the pot.

According to another legend, Chalchiuhtlicue was not Tláloc's wife but his sister. Tláloc's first wife was Xochiquetzal, the goddess of flowers and of "good love," but Tezcatlipoca stole her from him, as has already been related. Tláloc then took the goddess Matlalcueitl for his wife, "the lady of the green skirts," an ancient name for the Tlaxcalan mountain now known as Malinche.

This legend shows clearly the relationship that the Indians perceived as existing between the mountain ranges and the rains. It caused them to give the name of Tláloc to a mountain range, a name it still bears. According to the Aztecs, rain water was stored in great caves within the mountains, issuing later from springs. So it is that we commonly see in the hieroglyphic writings pictures of a hill with a cavern full of water within it.

Although Tláloc in general was a beneficent god, he had the power to unleash floods and send droughts, hail, ice, and lightning. Consequently he was also a god to be feared when angry; and in order to placate him and seek his favor, children especially were sacrificed to him and also prisoners dressed like the god.

There are many representations of Tláloc in sculptures, paintings, and on clay pots. It can be said that wherever there is a small isolated mound in the middle of a valley, there are certain to be found within it archaeological remains showing that the god of rain was worshiped there.

Tláloc is one of the most easily identified of the gods because of his characteristic mask, which, viewed from the front, gives him the appearance of wearing eyeglasses and a moustache. In one piece of sculp-

42

ture now in the Berlin Museum of Ethnography, it is apparent that in reality this mask is made up of two serpents intertwined to form a circle around the eyes, with the mouths of the serpents meeting above the mouth of the god.

The characteristic mask of Tláloc, as well as almost all his garments, is painted blue, the color of water against the sky, thereby representing the clouds. Tláloc's face and body are generally painted black, since he primarily represented the storm clouds; on the other hand, white clouds are symbolized by the heron-feather headdress, *aztatzontli,* which he wears on the crown of his head.

Chalchiuhtlicue *(Codex Borbonicus* 5).

43

Centéotl (*Codex Borgia* 14).

In the picture reproduced here, he is shown holding a flowering staff in one hand and sitting on a jade seat; raindrops falling from the sky form the background. On the nape of the neck he wears the pleated paper fan referred to earlier; on his head there is a conspicuous jewel, tipped with two quetzal feathers, called the *quetzalmiahuayo,* "the precious blade," signifying maize, which is so dependent on the god of rain.

His companion is the goddess of the sea and lakes, Chalchiuhtlicue, "the lady of the jade skirts." Her attire consists mainly of ornaments of paper made from the *amate,*[1] painted blue and white and tinted with melted rubber. The blue and white band with two large tassels, one hanging down on each side of the face, is an ever recurring feature in portrayals of this goddess. Her head is found on a green stone mask now in the National Museum of Mexico, but on the reverse side is her complete figure. Thanks to this piece, we know her calendar name was "Eight Malinalli," or "Eight Grass." Because this goddess was the special patroness of the sea, *huéyatl,* the Mexicans called the Gulf of Mexico, primarily the Veracruz region, Chalchiuhcueyécatl, "the water of the goddess Chalchiuhtlicue, or Chalchiuhcueye." Sahagún tells us that all those who had dealings with or whose livelihood depended upon the water, such as fishermen, makers of objects of tule, etc., prayed to her constantly.

On the other hand, those who traded in salt had a special goddess called Huixtocíhuatl, none other than the goddess of water, as can be seen from the details of her attire, although in her case the color blue

[1] Also *amatl* and *amatle,* a tree (*Ficus cotinifolia*), the bark of which was used to make paper in ancient times.

has been substituted for white. From existing data we do not know enough about the relationship of the goddess Huixtocíhuatl to Chalchiuhtlicue and Tláloc to say definitely that she is either the sister or the daughter of both of these gods. A similar situation exists in regard to Nappatecuhtli, "the lord of straw," god of those who made straw mats and other objects woven from rushes in the lagoons.

Huixtocíhuatl
(*Codex Matritense* VIII, 21).

Chicomecóatl, "Seven Serpent," is without doubt the most important of all the gods of vegetation. Consequently, the old chroniclers called her "the goddess of sustenance." She was also called "seven ears of corn," Chicomolotzin. In this connection, a piece of sculpture in the form of a rattlesnake, discovered a few years ago in the foundation work of the National Palace in Mexico City, is of great importance. It has a peculiar decoration of seven ears of corn on its body, which would certainly lead us to believe that it is a representation of Chicomecóatl.

Her cult was very ancient and probably came from the archaic era. As a goddess of fertility of the earth, she was also very naturally regarded as the goddess of human fertility, although in this form she was known by another name.

It is curious to observe that in the esoteric language of sorcerers and fortunetellers those calendar names that have the numeral "7" signify seeds. For example, "7 Serpent" is the esoteric name of corn, "7 Eagle" is the name of the squash seed, and so on. As a result, fortunetellers considered the number 7 as an omen of good luck, and anyone born on a day having this number would be lucky in life.

45

The goddess appears in the codices with her body and face painted red, and she wears a kind of paper mitre decorated with rosettes of the same material. In sculpture she also occasionally wears this adornment and in each hand holds a double ear of corn.

Even though Chicomecóatl was the general goddess of sustenance, the Aztecs converted each plant important to them into a god. Of course, for them, corn was the most important of all and was represented by a whole series of gods. Centéotl—literally *centli,* "corn," and *téotl,* "god," therefore, "god of corn"—was this plant deified.

Xilonen (*Codex Magliabecchiano* 24).

46

But if Centéotl was the corn god, generally speaking, the seed itself was thought of as a woman who represented in the various stages of her life the development of the ear of corn. Thus Xilonen was the tender ear of corn, or green corn, while Ilamatecuhtli, "the lady of the old skirt," was the dry ear, covered now by the yellow, wrinkled shucks.

Xilonen is one of the many deities borrowed by the Aztecs from other peoples. On earth, her part was taken by a young slave girl who was carried on the shoulders of a priest. The girl's head was cut off during one of the monthly festivals, signifying thus that the ear of corn had been severed from the stalk.

Xochipilli, "the prince of flowers," the patron of dances, games, and love, and symbol of summer, was intimately connected with Centéotl. He is sometimes thought to be related to the Red Tezcatlipoca, although the latter was more of a solar deity. His symbol, the *tonallo*, is formed by four points signifying the heat of the sun. Xochipilli is pictured adorned with flowers and butterflies, and he carries a staff, the *yolotopilli*, on which a human heart is impaled. A deity so similar to him that perhaps it is only his calendar name was "Five Flower," Macuilxóchitl, also the patron of games, dances, and sports. His wife Xochiquetzal, "the flower of the rich plume," was the personification of beauty and love. She was the goddess of flowers and the patroness of domestic work, but she was also the patroness of courtesans, the *auianime* or *maqui*, who lived with the bachelor warriors, because she had been kidnapped by the young Tezcatlipoca, the warrior from the North. She is characterized primarily by two large, erect panaches made from the feathers of the quetzal bird and by her richly embroidered garments.

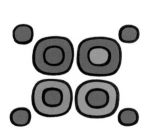

Xochipilli and Xochiquetzal were worshiped principally by the Indians of the *chinampas*, or floating gardens. They were the Xochimilcans, who then, as now grew on their floating gardens flowers used by the temples and palaces of Tenochtitlán.

The maguey (agave) plant was of great importance in the life of the Aztecs, not only

The glyph *tonallo (Codex Magliabecchiano,* blanket "of five roses").

Xochiquetzal

for the pulque *(octli)* which they extracted from it, but also for the many industrial products from the leaves and spines of the plant. It was deified under the name of Mayahuel. She was a goddess, who, like Venus of Ephesus, had four hundred breasts to nurse her four hundred children, the Centzon Totochtin, the four hundred or un-numbered gods of drunkenness. They were worshiped by various peoples of the Highlands and derived their names from the tribes whose patrons they were.

The most important of these was Ome-tochtli, "Two Rabbit," general god of pulque, but there are other gods. Tepoztécatl, worshiped in Tepoztlán, Morelos, is very important because of the series of myths centered about him. They have come down to us by word of mouth and are still told today in Tepoztlán, where the old myths are intermingled with Christian ideas and institutions and even with contemporary facts and happenings. Some legends say that this god, like Huitzilopochtli and Quetzalcóatl, was born of a virgin who conceived in a miraculous way. The story of a miraculous conception is repeated not only in the

A stone *teponaztle* (a horizontal cylindrical drum with slots on the top and sides which form two tongues) with the mask of Macuilxóchitl and Xochipilli (*Codex Magliabecchiano* 23).

Xochipilli (*Codex Magliabecchiano* 23).

Mayan myths, but also in accounts of a great number of the religions of the world, in which a miraculous conception almost constitutes a rule to explain the birth of a hero or god.

The husband of Mayahuel is Patécatl, who originally represented certain plants added to the pulque to aid fermentation. Later, however, he was transformed into one of the gods of medicine, for it was he who was used to "cure" the pulque and change it into a drink with magic and intoxicating power.

Finally, the god Xipe Tótec, "our lord the flayed one," is the god of spring and of jewelers. His cult was probably brought into the Valley of Mexico very early, since he is found in Teotihuacán culture, in which the so-called "god with a mask" is only a representation of Xipe. He was likewise called Yopi, and many of the ornaments worn by this god

49

Mayahuel (*Codex Borbonicus* 8).

are designated by this name. For example, his conical headdress is called *yopitzontli,* which would lead us to believe that he may have originated somewhere in the border region between the present-day states of Oaxaca and Guerrero, where there is a group of people called Tlapanecs or Yopis.

His cult is one of those most repugnant to our sensibilities, for it consisted in flaying a slave and covering a priest of the earth with the skin of the victim. This rite signified that when spring arrives, the earth must cover itself with a new coat of vegetation and exchange its dead skin for a new one.

In appearance, Xipe greatly resembles Tezcatlipoca, except, as has been said, he is a red Tezcatlipoca instead of a black one. All his clothes and adornments are red, and his face is painted with red and yellow horizontal stripes. His *nahual,* or disguise, is the *tlauhquéchol,* or spoon bird.

Various other gods closely associated with water and vegetation were represented in the Aztec pantheon, but many were only variations of those mentioned and their worship was less widespread and of less importance.

Xipe (*Codex Borbonicus* 14).

Tlaltecuhtli (*Codex Borbonicus* 16).

THE EARTH GODS

THE EARTH and death were very closely associated in the Aztec mind, not only because the earth is the place where the bodies of men are placed when they die, but also because it is the place where the stars hide; that is, the gods, when they fall in the West and descend to the world of the dead.

For the Mexican, the earth was a kind of monster, part shark and part alligator. Perhaps it was the so-called "alligator fish" from the rivers of the Gulf. It was also pictured as a fantastic frog whose mouth had great tusks and whose feet and hands were armed with claws. In

52

the form of a frog it was called Tlaltecuhtli and was considered a male, while in all other forms it was always a goddess.

In noting the connection that existed between the gods of the earth and the gods of night and death, we see that Tlaltecuhtli wears his hair curled in the same fashion as the infernal deities who rule over the world of the dead, and who will be described later. Moreover, centipedes, scorpions, spiders, serpents, and other nocturnal and poisonous creatures which were constant companions of the gods of death generally are shown in the god's hair.

Three goddesses, who apparently are only three different aspects of the same deity, portrayed the earth in its dual function of creator and destroyer: Coatlicue, Cihuacóatl, and Tlazoltéotl. Their names mean, respectively, "the lady of the skirt of serpents," "the serpent woman," and "the goddess of filth."

Coatlicue has a very important place in Aztec myths because she was the mother of the gods, that is, of the sun, the moon, and the stars. We have seen that she gave miraculous birth to Huitzilopochtli at the very moment when the stars, led by the moon, doubting the miracle of divine conception, attempted to kill her. We have also seen that the sun, Huitzilopochtli, sprang forth from her womb armed with a ray of light and killed the moon and the stars.

Aztec art, with all the barbaric originality of a young and energetic people, produced a masterpiece when it portrayed this goddess. The colossal statue of Coatlicue in the National Museum of Mexico surpasses in expressive force the more refined creations of peoples like the Mayas, whose concepts of life and the gods were expressed in more serene forms.

In accordance with her name, Coatlicue wears a skirt fashioned of braided serpents which is secured by another serpent in the form of a belt. A necklace of alternating human hands and hearts with a human skull or death's head as a pendant partially covers the goddess's breast. Her feet and hands are armed with claws, since she is the insatiable deity who feeds on the corpses of men. That is why she was also called "the devourer of filth." Her breasts hang flaccid, for she has nursed both the gods and mankind, since they are all her children. Hence she was known at Tonantzin, "our mother," Teteoinan, "the mother of the gods," and

Toci, "our grandmother." Her head has been severed from her body, and from the neck flow two streams of blood which take the form of two serpents portrayed in profile, their touching heads forming a fantastic face. Down the back of the goddess hangs an ornament of strips of red leather tipped with small shells, the decoration characteristic of earth gods.

The whole figure is an admirable synthesis of the ideas of love and destruction which correspond to the earth. In this piece of sculpture the Indian artist achieved to a supreme degree what in our concept of indigenous art is its enduring characteristic: reality in detail and subjectivity of the whole.

The figure does not represent a being but an idea, yet the parts show an amazing realism. The scales on the bodies of the serpents, the details of the macabre necklace, and the folds of the leather strips which form the back ornament have all been reproduced with a fidelity that can be found only in a people very close to nature.

Cihuacóatl is another name for this goddess, and she was the patron of the *cihuateteo*, the women who had died in childbirth, who wailed and moaned in the night air. They descended to the earth on certain days which were dedicated to them in the calendar, to appear at crossroads, and they were fatal to children. Subsequently Cihuacóatl has been transformed into *La Llorona*, "the weeping woman," of our popular Mexican folk tale. She is said to carry a cradle or the body of a dead child in her arms and to weep at night at the crossings of city streets. In times gone by, people knew that she had passed that way when they found in the market the empty cradle with a sacrificial knife laid beside it.

Tlazoltéotl, or Ixcuina, "the goddess of filthy things," was of more importance in the Aztec religion. It is thought that worship of her was brought from the Huastec region. Like Xipe, she is often portrayed as covered with the skin of a sacrificial victim. She can be easily identified by the band of raw cotton which she wears on her headdress and which is decorated with two spindles or bobbins. A black spot covers her nose and mouth. At times she carries a broom in her hand, "during the month that one sweeps," *Ochpaniztli,* when the principal ceremonies dedicated to her worship were celebrated. Her son is Centéotl, god of corn.

54

Tlazoltéotl (*Codex Borbonicus* 13).

Since she was the devourer of filth, she consumed the sins of men, thereby cleansing them of their impurities. Hence, the confessional rite that was practiced before the priests of Tlazoltéotl.

The priesthood of this goddess was of special importance. Cihuacóatl was the patron of childbirth and newborn children. It was the duty of her representatives to read the horoscopes of the newborn babies. These readings were based on the complicated combinations of the ritual calendar, the *tonalpohualli*. Special priests called *tonalpouque* exercised this function and gave a name to the child according to the day of his birth. They recorded these matters in hieroglyphic script in special books called *tonalámatl,* which were folded in the form of a screen, several of which have been preserved. Tlazoltéotl's priests, also priests of the earth and of fertility, were very important in the Aztec cult and are frequently pictured in the indigenous manuscripts that have been handed down to us.

THE GODS OF DEATH

NOTWITHSTANDING the similarity of the concepts of night, earth, and death, as opposed to those of light, sky, and life, there were special deities who held dominion over the underworld, which the Aztecs thought of as the dwelling place of those who had died. It was called *Mictlan,* the place where Mictlantecuhtli, "the lord of the dead," ruled.

The god is portrayed with his body covered with human bones. Over his face he wears a mask in the form of a human skull. His hair is black, curled, and studded with starlike eyes, since he dwells in a region of utter darkness. He wears paper ornaments in the form of rosettes, with cones protruding from the center; one is worn over the forehead, the other on the back of the neck. They are called *ixcochtechimalli* and *cuechcochtechimalli* respectively and are typical of his attire. He uses a human bone as an earplug. Animals associated with him are the bat,

56

Mictlantecuhtli *(Codex Borbonicus* 10).

the spider, and the owl *(tecólotl)*, a bird of ill omen whose nocturnal song is considered even today to be fatal to anyone who hears it.

THE PARADISES
AND THE HELLS

WHERE A MAN'S SOUL went after death was not determined by his conduct in this life, according to the Aztecs, but rather by the manner of his death and his occupation in life.

The eastern and the western paradises of the sun have already been discussed. To the first, called *Tonatiuhichan,* "the house of the sun," went the souls of warriors who fell in combat or who died victims on the sacrificial stone. In gardens filled with flowers they are the daily companions of the sun, they fight sham battles, and when the sun rises in the East, they greet him with great shouts of joy and beat their shields loudly. When they return to earth after four years, they are transformed into hummingbirds and other birds with exotic plumage and feed upon the nectar of flowers. They are the privileged ones whom the sun has chosen for his retinue and live a life of pure delight.

> The ancient ones said that the Sun calls them unto him so that they can live there in the sky with him, so that they can gladden his heart and sing in his presence and give him pleasure; they share a life of continued delight with him, they enjoy constant pleasures and taste and sip the nectar of all sweet-tasting and sweet-smelling flowers; never do they feel sad or experience any pain or sorrow, because they live in the mansion of the Sun, where there is an abundance of delights; and those who die in combat are honored in this manner here in this world, and this way of meeting death is much desired by many, and many envy those who so died and for that reason desire this death, since those who so die are held in great esteem.[1]

[1] Sahagún, *Historia general de las Cosas de Nueva España,* II, 140. Bernardino Sahagún, also known as Bernardino Ribeira (1499?–1590), was a Franciscan friar

Even the enemy warriors who died in combat or who were taken prisoners and sacrificed on the *téchcatl,* the sacrificial stone, were honored in this paradise. For them there was a special god called Teoyaomiqui, whose name means "the god of the enemy dead."

They were the ones who had been sacrificed to the sun, the men-stars, who, when they died, gave their lives to nourish the powerful warrior who does battle in the sky. For that reason they were the equal of the Aztecs who died in combat.

> It is related that a generous young man from Huexotzinco, called Mixcóatl, died in combat with the Mexicans and that they killed him in battle, and so goes a song in his praise: "Oh, blessed Mixcóatl, well dost thou deserve to be praised in song and well dost thou deserve thy fame to be remembered in the world and well dost thou deserve that those who dance the *areitos* bring thee in their mouth, around the large drums and the small drums, so that you may appear and gladden the hearts of the noble and generous ones, thy relatives. Oh generous youth, worthy of all praise, who offered thy heart to the sun, clean as a string of sapphires, again thou wilt blossom forth and flower in the world and thou wilt come when the *areito* is sung and danced and among the large drums and the small drums of Huexotzinco wilt thou appear to the nobles and valiant men, and thy friends shall see thee.[2]

Women who died in childbirth dwelled in the western paradise, called *Cincalco,* "the house of corn," where they occupied a prominent place. When they returned to earth, they did so at night, when they became frightful phantoms of ill omen, especially for women and young children. They were the *cihuateteo,* "the goddess-women," who are pictured as fearsome creatures with a skull for a head and hands and feet tipped with claws. However, before she became a goddess, a woman who died in childbirth had great magical power, since she had been the

born in Sahagún, Spain. He came to Mexico in 1529, only eight years after the conquest of Mexico City. He studied the Indian languages and collected the myths, legends, and traditions of the Indians from his Indian pupils and elders of the tribe. He became one of the New World's first anthropologists, linguists, and educators. His monumental work was not published until 1829, in Mexico. It is still one of the best sources of information on the Aztecs.

[2] *Ibid.,* II, 140.

strong one who defeated the enemy. Young warriors tried to get possession of her right arm, because it would make them invincible in battle. That is why, when a woman who died in childbirth was buried, the funeral cortege was surrounded by the men of her clan, armed to the hilt. They had spent the entire night watching at the side of the dead woman to prevent ambitious young men from mutilating the corpse.

Those who died by drowning, by lightning, from leprosy or any other illness considered related to the water gods, went to Tlalocan, the paradise of Tláloc. Located in the South, it was the place of fertility, where all kinds of fruit trees grew, where corn, beans, *chia,*[3] and all other foodstuffs abounded.

From several magnificent paintings recently discovered in a temple at Teotihuacán, we can deduce that since the Teotihuacán epoch, that is, since approximately the sixth century after Christ, there had existed the idea of a place of delight, the Tlalocan, to which the dead repaired. These paintings illustrate what Sahagún relates in his history. A dry bough was placed on the tomb at the burial of the one who had been chosen by the rain god and who had died from any of the aforementioned diseases, or by an accident in the water, or by lightning. When the fortunate one reached the Elysian fields, that is, Tlalocan, the dry bough became green again, indicating that in this place of abundance he acquired a new life. After intoning a long song, no doubt of thanks to the god who makes all things grow, he joined his companions to enjoy a life of eternal happiness spent lolling beneath the trees heavy with fruit on the banks of the rivers of paradise; or he submerged in the waters of the lagoons far beyond death and passed the time singing with his companions, joining in their games, and sharing their pleasures. The life of those who had been summoned by Tláloc was conceived of by the Aztecs, and before them the Teotihuacáns, as one of abundance, serenity, and blessedness.

But those not selected by either the sun or Tláloc merely went to Mictlan, which lies in the North. There the souls of the dead underwent a series of magical trials as they passed through several hells.

There were nine of these in which the soul must suffer before it reached, after a period of four years, its final rest.

[3] A salvia used for seasoning food.

60

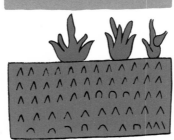

The nine hells and the thirteen heavens
(*Codex Vaticanus* A).

In the first place, in order to reach Mictlan, the dead must cross a deep river, the Chignahuapan, which was the first of the trials to which the gods of the underworld subjected them. Thus a tawny-haired dog was buried with the dead, so that it could help its master cross the river. In the second realm, the soul had to pass between two mountains that were joined together; in the third, it must climb over a mountain of obsidian; in the fourth, the soul was subjected to an icy wind, so bitter that it cut like obsidian knives; in the fifth realm, the soul must pass through a place where flags waved; in the sixth, it was pierced by arrows; in the seventh hell were wild beasts that ate human hearts; in the eighth, the soul must pass over narrow paths between stones; and in the ninth and final hell, the Chignahumictlan, the souls found repose or disappeared forever.

A variety of amulets or charms were buried with the dead in order to help him endure the magical trials in the other world. He was given a jug of water for the journey, and his body was wrapped in a winding sheet in a squatting position, tightly secured with blankets and papers. Other papers helped him to pass through the clashing mountains, or the place guarded by the great snake, or where the green lizard called Xochitónal lay in wait, or over the nine bleak plains, Chicunaixtlahuaca, and over the nine hills. The garments that the deceased had worn in this life were burned, so that he would feel no cold when he passed through the place where the wind blew so cold it cut like a knife; a jade bead was placed in his mouth to serve as his heart, which he would doubtless leave as a pawn in the seventh hell, where the wild beasts devoured the hearts of men. And, finally, certain valuable objects were placed with the dead to be presented to Mictlantecuhtli or Mictecacíhuatl when he should reach the end of his journey. Then the corpse and its effects were burned. The ashes and the jade bead were kept in an urn buried in one of the rooms of the house. Offerings were made to them eighty days after the burial, and thereafter once every year until the four years required for the journey to the beyond were over. After that, no further offerings were made.

Many were the gods and goddesses who lived in the various regions of the Aztec underworld. The most important were Mictlantecuhtli and Mictecacíhuatl, "the lord and mistress of the underworld." Appar-

62

Mictecacíhuatl *(Codex Fejérvary-Mayer* 28).

ently they dwelled in the ninth realm, or the deepest of the subterranean chambers, known as the Chignahumictlan. But there were other gods of the dead who always appear in pairs, a god and a goddess who seem to have had dominion over the other parts of the underworld not quite so deep as that over which the first ruled.

Several of the names of these deities have come down to us; for example, Ixpuzteque, "he of the broken foot," and his wife, Nesoxochi, "the one who strews flowers." Another god is Nextepeua, "he who rains ashes," and his wife is Micapetlacalli, "the box of death." A third is called Tzontémoc, "he who fell head first," and his wife, Chalmecacíhuatl, "the sacrificer." And, finally we know that another of the gods of death was called Acolnahuácatl, "the one from the twisted region," but we do not know the name of his wife. These pairs of infernal gods remind us of those mentioned in the *Popol Vuh,* the sacred book of the Quiché Mayas, when the heroes Hunahpú and Xbalanqué—descendants, on the maternal side, of one of the gods of the underworld—set out on the road to the infernal regions. When they arrived at the crossroads, they left the roads marked white, red, and green, which went to other regions, and took the road marked black, which led to Xibalbá. There they found the fourteen gods of the underworld, who were also divided into pairs.

There is also evidence of the existence of thirteen heavens, but we are not told that the souls of men went there.

In the highest heaven, which was the double heaven, lived Ometecuhtli and Omecíhuatl, the creator gods. The souls of children who died before they reached the age of reason dwelled there. There, too, were men's souls engendered, nourished by a tree that gave forth milk. They are waiting until the present human race is destroyed in the final cataclysm; then they will be reincarnated in a new human race.

Beneath this double heaven, which we should call the twelfth and thirteenth heavens, was the eleventh heaven, which was red. Beneath it was the tenth, which was yellow, and beneath it was the ninth, which was white. It is said that in the eighth heaven the obsidian knives were rattled. The seventh heaven, which was blue, was the abode of Huitzilopochtli. Hence his temple on the great pyramid of Mexico was called *Ilhuícatl Xoxouqui,* or "blue heaven." The sixth was green; and in the fifth were errant stars, comets, and fire. In the fourth lived Huixtocíhuatl, "the goddess of salt," who has already been mentioned. The third was the heaven through which the sun traveled; in the second were the stars, and there also lived Citlalatónac, the Milky Way, and Citlalicue, gods of the night sky, as well as the goddess who had the name "skirt of stars." And, finally, in the first heaven, that is, the one nearest the earth, the moon followed her course and the clouds formed.

The thirteen celestial gods who lived in the thirteen heavens and the nine lords of the underworld occupied a position of great importance in the calendar and gave their benevolent or evil character to the days with which they were associated.

THE CALENDARS

THE AZTECS had two calendars that determined their religious ceremonies. The most important was the one called *tonalpohualli*. It was a combination of a series of twenty signs with another series of numbers from 1 to 13, the signs and the numbers being combined in such a way that both series followed an invariable order. The same combination of sign and number was not repeated until 13 times 20 or 260 days had passed.

The series of signs is as follows:

Alligator	Monkey
Wind	Grass
House	Reed
Lizard	Jaguar
Serpent	Eagle
Death	King Buzzard (vulture)
Deer	Earthquake
Rabbit	Flint (knife)
Water	Rain
Dog	Flower

The series of the thirteen numbers follows the normal order: 1, 2, 3, 4, 5, 6, 7, 8, 9, 10, 11, 12, 13.

By combining both series, one gets "1 Alligator" as the name of the first day; of the second, "2 Wind"; of the third, "3 House"—until one reaches the day "13 Reed." The following day is called "1 Jaguar"; the next, "2 Eagle," and so on. When the day "Flower" is reached, it is necessary to start counting the day "Alligator" over again with its corresponding number.

This ritual calendar, or *tonalpohualli,* is one of the most original developments of the indigenous cultures of Mesoamerica. It is very ancient, for we find it already in use in Oaxaca at the time of the first culture that flourished in the valley, several centuries before the Christian era, and that is known to us as Monte Albán I. This calendar was essentially the basis for all the other calendar computations, such as the Mayan, the Zapotec, the Mixtec, the Totonac, the Huaxtec, the Teotihuacán, the Toltec, and the Aztec.

All the peoples of Mesoamerica were familiar with and used this calendar, and the day known in Mexico, for example, by the name "13 Serpent" was likewise known by a similar or corresponding name in the entire Mesoamerican area from Pánuco to Nicaragua and from Sinaloa to Yucatán.

The period of the 260 days, or the *tonalpohualli,* was recorded in special books called *tonalámatl,* "paper or book of the days." Hence the priests who interpreted its signs and the succession of events according to the propitious days and the evil days were known as the *tonalpouque.*

We do not know where this ritual calendar originated. It is so important and so characteristic of Mexico and Central America that the Mesoamerican zone could be called the zone of the *tonalpohualli.* Its development is without doubt very old, and it must have been the creation of a people who attained a high degree of culture prior to that of all the peoples with whose cultures we are now familiar.

This period of 260 days, consisting of different names, according to the number or the sign, was a magic period that helped the Aztec astrologers predict and avoid the evil fortune that befell a man born on a day of evil omen, for a child was given the name of the day on which he was born. But since the gods also took the names of the days on which they were born or of those on which they had performed some important deed that was to be commemorated, the ceremonies celebrated for this reason took place each 260 days, that is, when the name of the day in the *tonalpohualli* was repeated again.

The ceremony in honor of the sun is particularly notable. It fell on the day called "4 Movement" or "Earthquake" and commemorated the day on which the sun was to be destroyed by earthquakes, as was explained in the discussion of the creation of the present sun.

This festival probably took place before the stone we now know by the name of the Aztec Calendar, in an edifice called *Quauhxicalco*. One of the prisoners of war, whose body was painted like that of the stellar gods, white with red stripes, *huahuantin,* was given a staff, a buckler, and a bundle containing eagle feathers and white paintings. He was then led to the temple, where, just before he mounted the steps, the people besought him to take all these objects to the sun as a gift and implored him to pray for the health and good fortune of the Mexican people. Then the captive began slowly to ascend the temple steps, pausing on each step to symbolize the passage of the sun. On his arrival at the summit of the temple he was sacrificed by the priests, who tore out his heart and offered it to the sun. On that day all the people practiced the rite of self-sacrifice by pricking blood from their ears or from other parts of their bodies and observing a rigorous fast until midday. In the afternoon the nobles danced, adorned in their best finery, for this was a festival of the nobles and particularly of the military orders of the eagles and the jaguars, two orders dedicated to the worship of the sun.

The Aztecs considered the calendar day called "1 Serpent" especially lucky and prosperous. It was believed to be favorable to merchants and traders, especially those who traveled in foreign lands selling and buying merchandise, who were called *pochtecas*. Because of this belief, merchants waited until the day "1 Serpent" to set out on commercial expeditions. When this day arrived, they held a great banquet to which they invited the elder merchants, known as *pochtecatlatohque,* and the most distinguished men of their clan, the *calpulli,* to whom they disclosed their plans for the trip.

When the banquet was over, the elder merchants arose and counseled them how to proceed. They told of the dangers and the hardships of the business, at the same time pointing out the advantages of wealth and honor that it brought. One merchant then arose and delivered an elegant discourse in answer to the old men. He thanked them for the words that they had spoken, "words taken from the treasure that you guard in your hearts, words that are beautiful as gold and precious stones and rich feathers," and as such he received them and esteemed them.

Then there began for the family of the traveling trader a period of mourning. Only once every four months could they wash their heads and faces, although they were allowed to bathe their bodies. If the merchant died on the road, within four days after receipt of the death message they could bathe and wash their faces. If he had died at the hands of an enemy, they made an image of sticks, tied together and decked with papers and other ornaments used for this purpose. Then they took the image to the temple of the *calpulli* to which the merchant belonged; there it was left for a whole day while the family stood before it lamenting the departed. At midnight they removed the statue and placed it in the courtyard of the temple, where it was burned. This concluded the ceremonies in honor of the deceased.

The majority of the festivals and religious ceremonies, however, were regulated by the annual calendar, which was divided into eighteen months of twenty days each, plus five additional days called *nemontemi*. Since the latter were considered days of ill omen, no festivals were held on those days.

As the months were dedicated to the major deities, the ceremonies held each month varied, although they generally had as their purpose the symbolic portrayal of the life or birth of a god. In this manner the Aztecs besought the god to continue his favors.

Naturally, since the annual calendar was an agricultural calendar, many of these festivals were held in honor of Tláloc or the deities of vegetation. There were others, however, dedicated to Huitzilopochtli, to Tezcatlipoca, and to other major gods.

A ceremony interesting because of its symbolism took place in the sixth month, called *Tóxcatl*. A young warrior who had been captured in battle was selected as a symbol or incarnation of the god Tezcatlipoca. For one whole year the priests taught him how to conduct himself as a personage of the court by instructing him in the manners of a noble.

They also taught him to play the clay flutes and gave him a select entourage to accompany him and attend to his wants as if he were a lord. Dressed in the attire of the god, he strolled through the city streets carrying a bouquet of flowers in the manner of the nobles and smoking tobacco from a richly gilded reed pipe. Whoever met this living representation of Tezcatlipoca paid him great reverence and held him in as much esteem as if he were the king himself.

At the beginning of the month of *Tóxcatl,* or twenty days before the celebration of the festival, his dress was changed to that worn by the great captains and war lords. He was married to four young maidens called Xochiquetzal, Xilonen, Atlatonan, and Huixtocíhuatl, incarnations of the wives of the god of providence.

When the day of the festival arrived, great ceremonies, dances, and banquets were held in honor of the youth. Everyone, nobles as well as plebeians, honored and praised him as if his reign were to last forever.

On the day of the festival he, along with his new wives and court, was taken in one of the royal canoes to a small, neglected temple on the shore of a lake. Here, the wives who had been with him during the time of his prosperity left him, as did the brilliant entourage that had kept him company. Now, almost alone, with only a few pages, he began to walk toward the temple, carrying in his hands the clay flutes which he had played when he was regarded as a great lord.

At the temple steps even his pages abandoned him. Alone, he began the ascent, breaking one of the small flutes, a symbol of his past grandeur, on each of the temple steps.

Slowly he ascended the steps of the temple. When he arrived at the summit, the priests were already awaiting him. Stripping him of his last finery, they stretched him out on the sacrificial stone and tore out his heart. "They said," Sahagún tells us, "that this signifies that those who enjoy wealth and pleasures in this life will end in poverty and in sorrow."

As soon as this youth had died, another was chosen to represent the god, and he, too, was regaled and cared for in the same way until the following year when the month of *Tóxcatl* returned, bringing with it the end of his life.

Another ceremony, curious because of the resemblance it bears to

69

certain popular European festivals, was celebrated during the month of *Xocotlhuetzi.*

During the preceding month the people went into the forest and cut a very tall tree, approximately fifteen meters in height, perfectly straight and so great in circumference that a man could not reach around it.

With much ceremony they brought this tree, called *xócotl,* from the forest, dancing and singing to it as if it were a god, carrying it upon other logs so that the bark would not be injured. When they drew near the city, the women of the nobility came out to receive them, with jugs of chocolate and with garlands of flowers which they hung upon the necks of the bearers.

Later they dug a hole in the plaza and set the *xócotl* in it. On the upper part of the trunk they tied two logs together to form a cross, and from the seed of the amaranth tree they made an image of the god. They clothed the image in white paper garments and decorations, and these great strips of paper of varying length fluttered in the breeze like pennants. Also hanging from the tree were heavy ropes which reached almost to the base.

When all the other ceremonies for the month of *Xocotlhuetzi* were completed, the people ran to the plaza where the tree stood. At its foot the leaders of the young men were stationed to prevent anyone from getting a head start, beating off the boldest to keep them from taking advantage of their companions. But when the signal was given for the game to begin, all the youths rushed forward as one and tried to climb the ropes to the top of the trunk where the amaranth-seed image of the god had been placed.

Veritable clusters of youths hung from each rope, for all were eager to attain the great honor of reaching the image first. Those who were shrewd waited until the ropes were swarming with men and then, climbing up over the shoulders of one after another, made their way to the highest point, reaching it ahead of the more impatient ones. The first youth to reach the top seized the idol, together with its shield, darts, dart hurler, and several large pieces of bread, or *tamales,* made from the same paste as the idol, and broke the image and the bread into small pieces and scattered them over the heads of the people in the plaza below. Everyone attempted to catch a piece, even though it was no more than

70

Dance of the Xocotlhuetzi (*Codex Borbonicus* 28).

a small bit of the dough from which the god was made, for it was to be eaten in the manner of taking communion. When the victor descended with the arms which he had taken from the god as from an enemy, the crowd below received him with loud cheers, and the old men took him to the top of the temple, where they presented him with jewels and other regalia. They placed on his shoulders a tawny-colored mantle bordered in rabbit fur and feathers which only men who had accomplished such a feat were permitted to wear publicly. Dressed in this fashion, the youth descended from the temple, surrounded by the priests, with the eldest in the lead. Amidst a warlike clamor made by the conch shell trumpets and accompanied by the whole cortege, he carried the shield he had taken from the image to his home, where he deposited it as evidence of his feat.

A detailed description of the festivals that were celebrated during the other months cannot be given here. Anyone interested in these celebrations should consult the extensive accounts by Sahagún and Durán.[1] But a brief résumé of the different forms of sacrifice performed by the ancient Mexicans will be made.

It has already been said that the essence of human sacrifice among the Aztecs lay in the conception of the interdependence of man and his gods. Human sacrifice was not performed for the purpose of harming the sacrificed, nor was cruelty or vengeance its objective. It was something more than that, as was made clear during the discussion of sacrifice to the sun. The victim was considered a messenger to the gods, bearing the supplications of the Aztec people; witness the rite of sacrifice in the month of *Tóxcatl,* in which the youth who represented Tezcatlipoca was treated and revered as if he himself were a god.

Human sacrifice among the Aztecs, however repugnant it may be to us, was nothing more than one of many such aberrations which assume a religious guise in the history of mankind, and which, based upon false premises considered valid, can lead quite logically to the most terrible consequences. Burning heretics in this life to save them from the everlasting fires of hell, destroying individuals of a supposedly inferior race

---

[1] Diego Durán (1537–88), a Dominican friar, born in Seville, Spain (?), lived in Texcoco from childhood. He finished his *Historia de las Indias de la Nueva España e Islas de Tierra Firme* in 1581. It was published in Mexico in 1867 and 1880.

to keep them from contaminating the Aryan, and the like, are examples of similar practices found frequently in the history of ideologies and religions.

Human sacrifice was practiced in various forms by the Aztecs. Ordinarily it consisted in placing the victim on a stone called *téchcatl,* similar in shape to a sugar loaf or cone with the top somewhat flattened out.

Four priests seized the victim by the arms and legs and laid him on his back on the *téchcatl* in such a way that his chest was arched upwards. Then a fifth priest took the flint knife and plunged it into the breast, thrust his hand into the open wound, tore out the heart, and offered it to the gods.

At other times, during the ceremonies in honor of the god Xipe, the prisoner was tied to the upper part of a kind of framework and then riddled by arrows until he died. The prisoner's blood spilling on the ground was thought to make it fertile and to stimulate by a sort of magical sympathy the fall of the other precious liquid, rain.

We have already discussed another type of sacrifice associated with Xipe and with the goddess of earth. In this rite the victim was flayed and the priest dressed in his skin. Decapitation and burning were also used as methods of sacrifice.

Gladiatorial sacrifice was reserved for those who had distinguished themselves by their valor. It consisted of a real duel between a prisoner captain and several of the most distinguished Aztec warriors, two of whom must be knights of the military Order of the Eagles and two of the Order of the Jaguars. It was not an equal fight, however, since the captive was bound, and to defend himself had only a wooden sword with small tufts of downy feathers attached to its edges instead of obsidian blades. His sponsor, or second, dressed like a bear, gave him four heavy sticks of pine to serve as spears to hurl at his enemies. The captive fought with one knight at a time. If the first should be defeated, another would take up the battle. If, in spite of his inferior weapons, the captive succeeded in vanquishing the four knights, a fifth, who was left-handed, generally killed him.

We are told, however, that a Tlaxcaltecan warrior named Tlahui-cole did succeed in defeating all five of the knights and was consequently

Gladiatorial sacrifice *(Codex Magliabecchiano* 18).

pardoned. Thereafter he was given command of the Aztec forces in a campaign against the Tarascan Indians. After the war was over, he chose to die and was finally sacrificed. His action clearly indicates that, since he had been taken captive in battle, he considered himself as a chosen one of the sun, and therefore could not attribute his defeat to natural causes. It was not his strength and valor that had failed him; rather, it was the manifest will of the god that caused him to be taken prisoner; and therefore he could not flee or free himself without thwarting the divine will.

A much discussed and very important aspect of the Aztec ritual was cannibalism, or the eating of the flesh of the victims. Did the Aztecs eat human flesh as food, or simply as a ritual ceremony? Undoubtedly Aztec cannibalism was a rite performed as a religious ceremony, so much so that he who had captured a prisoner could not eat his flesh, because the captive was looked upon as his son. It should not be forgotten that in the minds of the Aztecs the human victims were the very incarnation of the gods whom they represented and whose attire they wore, and when they ate their flesh, they were performing a kind of communion with the divinity, just as when they ate the pieces of Huitzilopochtli's image made from the seeds of the amaranth, they believed that their bodies would be mingled with that of the divine host and that they would miraculously receive the benefits of the communion.

Since we have already analyzed the bloody aspect of Aztec religious ceremonies, let us now examine their more pleasing manifestations. Worship of the gods also included hymns sung in the temples, dances, mock hunts and battles, games, masquerades, and theatrical performances.

Several sacred hymns sung in homage to the gods have come down to us; they either recall the glorious deeds or solicit the favor of the gods.

Songs dedicated to Huitzilopochtli, Tláloc, to the mother of the gods, to the god of fire, to Xochipilli, to Xochiquetzal, to Xipe Tótec, to the god of merchants, and others have been preserved. The following is a fragment of the song to Xipe Tótec, the god of spring.

Thou, night drinker,
Why must thou be coaxed?

Put on thy mask,
Put on thy golden garments.

Oh, my god, thy water of precious stones
Has fallen;
The tall cypress
Has changed into a quetzal bird.
The fire serpent
Has been changed into a plumed serpent.

The fire serpent has let me go free.
Perhaps he will disappear,
Perhaps he will disappear, and I will destroy myself,
I, the tender cornstalk.
Like unto the precious jade
My heart is green;
But I shall yet see the gold

And I shall rejoice if it has ripened,
If the leader of the war is born.

Oh, my god, cause
Some of the stalks of corn at least,
To bring forth grain in abundance;
Thy faithful follower turns his eyes towards thy mount,
Towards thee;
I shall rejoice if something ripens first, if I can say
That the leader of the war is born.

This song is an invocation to the god by the priest, who prays for rain, so that, as he says poetically, when the water of precious stones falls, the cypress will become as the feather of the quetzal bird, and the fire serpent, drought, will be changed into a serpent of precious plumes, or into green vegetation that will cover the earth. For that reason, the corn god, who depends on rain, makes this doleful supplication: "Perhaps he may disappear so that I may destroy myself, I, the tender stalk of corn." Later he says that his heart is still like a precious green stone, but that perhaps it will see the god, that is, it will grow into a yellow ear of corn.

Then, when the corn ripens into grain, a fragment of the hymn to Centéotl, the corn god, is sung:

The god of corn is born
In Tamoanchan.
In the place where there are flowers
The god "One Flower,"
The god of corn is born
In the place where there is water and moisture,
Where the sons of man are made,
In beautiful Michoacán.

These songs, which specialists in the Nahuatl language consider very difficult to translate, probably predate the Aztecs; they are likely of Toltec origin and are written in the esoteric language *nahuatlatolli*, which can only be made intelligible by a thorough knowledge of the myths and the indigenous religion.

Another form of ritual was the dance. The conquistadors and chron-

Aztec dance (*Codex Florentino* XXIII–19, musicians).

iclers who had the opportunity to observe them were greatly impressed by these native dances, which were sometimes performed by both men and women, sometimes by either men or women alone.

The dancers were arrayed in different costumes according to the ceremony. At times they wore jewelry of immense value, especially during the dances of the nobles. Pedro de Alvarado's[2] greed was so

[2] Pedro de Alvarado (1485?–1541) was a Spanish conquistador born in Badajoz, Spain. He was Cortés' right-hand man and most trusted lieutenant during the conquest of Mexico. He later conquered Guatemala and founded old Guatemala City. His brilliance as a leader and conquistador was marred by his excessive cruelty and greed.

Ball game *(Codex Magliabecchiano* 68).

aroused on such an occasion that he staged the famous massacre of *Tóxcatl,* one of his objectives being to seize the rich jewels worn by the Aztec nobles.

One of the most colorful dances was performed by many persons of different ages and ranks. The dancers formed a circle around a central altar, where an orchestra of drums, flutes, conch shell trumpets, and other kinds of timbrels was grouped. The oldest and most important people made up the first and inner circle, for their movements were slow and their steps measured. The farther away from the center a circle was, the less important and younger the dancers became, until the youngest formed the outside circle. This last group had to execute the dance steps with great speed in order not to lose their place in the circle.

In the ceremonies held in honor of Quetzalcóatl, theatrical pieces were used as a part of the worship of the god of wind. The actors took the parts of sick people making their way to the temple in search of health. They would invent dialogues which were amusing because of the physical defects of the people portrayed. Other actors disguised as animals related the stories of their lives, climbed up in trees, and were hunted by the priests. The sharp repartee between the hunters and the hunted caused laughter among the spectators. We have little information concerning these sketches, but they do indicate that a dramatic art had developed and was flourishing among the Mexicans and that, as usual, its origin was closely associated with religious observances.

Games and sports also played a part in ceremonies dedicated to the gods and hence had religious significance.

Among the most important of the sports was the ball game, which appears very early in the history of Mexico and Central America, for we find it being played in the cities of the classical age of the Mayans and among the old cultures of Oaxaca. Undoubtedly the Aztecs inherited this game from their predecessors.

It was played in special courts called *tlachtli,* laid out in the form of the letter "H," with the central bar longer than the laterals. The players used a solid rubber ball that could be struck only with the elbow, knee, or hip. The object of the game was to knock the ball from one field to another, driving it across the dividing line in the center of the court. But if one of the teams succeeded in knocking the ball through one of the two stone rings fixed to the lateral walls of the court, that team won the game, no matter how many points it had previously lost.

This solid rubber ball was so hard that a player struck by it might be seriously injured. Therefore, each member of the team wore a kind of leather apron and, to protect his stomach, a kind of leather belt stuffed with cotton. He wore a knee pad on the knee that touched the ground when he bent down to strike the ball with his hip or elbow, and he wore hard leather gloves to protect his hands when he had to rush to the ground to strike the ball. The impact of the ball was so great, many of the chroniclers tell us, that after the game was over the players' hips were so badly bruised from striking the ball that incisions had to be made with obsidian knives to drain the blood from the bruised areas.

This ball game was so important that certain Mixtec manuscripts show the great princes and kings in the ball court carrying gold and jade jewelry to wager on the game. In the *Popol Vuh* we are told that the

79

Patolli players praying to Macuilxóchitl (*Codex Magliabecchiano* 48). *Patolli* is a game of chance played on a board shaped like a cross, with rectangles marked off in the arms of the cross; the game has been compared to parchesi. Macuilxóchitl, the five-flower god of all games, was invoked by the players.

Quiché demi-gods defeated the gods of the underworld in a ball game in Xibalbá.

The game had religious significance and the ball court was in reality a temple. The ball symbolized a star, the sun, or the moon, or else the movement of the entire firmament. Among the edifices of the great Temple of Tenochtitlán mentioned by Sahagún, there were at least two such courts, dedicated to the sun and to the moon.

Another sport that had religious significance was the game we know by the name of *volador*. It is still played by the Totonacs of the northern part of the state of Veracruz.

This game required climbing a very tall, slick pole, near the top of which was fastened a square wooden frame. Each of the four players participating in this dangerous sport was tied to a corner of the framework. The four were dressed as macaws, birds sacred to the sun. A fifth individual stood atop the mast on a cylinder, which revolved as he played the flute. The four men tied to the corners of the frame jumped off at the same time, so that the ropes to which they were tied would unreel and cause the wooden cylinder on which the flute player stood to turn around and around. Each player whirled around the pole thirteen times, and on the last revolution, as soon as his feet touched the ground, he began running. The four macaws jumping from the pole and whirling around it thirteen times are symbolic of the fifty-two years that make up the Aztec cycle of years, that is, the movement of the sun in the thirteen-multiplied-by-four revolutions which equal fifty-two years.

Also symbolic of the fifty-two-year cycle is a game of dice similar to "royal goose," which was played with beans having certain markings or with split reeds that were marked on the concave side. Known as *patolli,* this game was dedicated to Macuilxóchitl and Ometochtli. In addition to its astronomical significance, it had a religious character, as is indicated by the invocation made while it was being played.

The ancient Mexicans performed many other religious and magic ceremonies on the occasion of births, baptisms, puberty, marriages, and deaths, and whenever they undertook a public or private business enterprise. But the limitations of this book do not allow us to dwell further on that subject.

PRIESTLY ORGANIZATION

SINCE RELIGION encompassed the entire life of the Aztecs, individually as well as collectively, we can assume that every Mexican performed, in some way or another, certain priestly functions, since he was obliged to execute certain rites of the cult.

Even the highest functionaries of the Aztec city had a dual capacity, one priestly and one military, a common trait in the social organization of the Mexicans. Thus the *Tlacatecuhtli,* or *Tlatoani,* whom the

esta zpintura cō
ojos significa
la noche

alfaqui major (esta de no
che mirando las estre
llas enel cielo zqaber
la coza que es / que tie
ne zqur fofz congo /.

A priest contemplating the stars
(*Codex Mendocino* or *Codex Mendoza* 63).

Spaniards called the emperor, and the *Cihuacóatl,* next in rank, were charged with important priestly functions.

There existed, however, a large class of priests and priestesses, specialists in the cult of the gods and in the multiple duties originating from such worship.

At the apex of the hierarchy stood two major priests. They were the *Quetzalcóatl-Totec tlamacazqui* and the *Quetzalcóatl-Tláloc tlamacazqui.* The former was the representative of the patron god of the city, Huitzilopochtli; the second, of Tláloc, the rain god. These two gods were the only ones whose sanctuaries were on the highest pyramid of the Great Temple. The name Quetzalcóatl was given to both priests, commemorating the god whom the Mexicans looked upon as the prototype priest.

It is interesting to note that not only in Mexico but also in other

82

places, such as Cholula and Cempoala, these two priests held the supreme rank. This indicates perhaps that, as in the case of Tenochtitlán, there were two gods who shared equally the veneration of the people. It does not, however, seem to be an original Aztec idea, for there was in Tenayuca a temple with two sanctuaries on the highest platform.

Immediately below the two priests of Huitzilopochtli and Tláloc in rank was the so-called *Mexícatl Teohuatzin,* who was in charge of the religious affairs of Tenochtitlán and the conquered provinces. He was likewise the immediate superior of the other priests.

His assistants were the *Huitznáhuac Teohuatzin* and the *Tepanteohuatzin,* or *Tecpanteohuatzin* (?), who seems to have been a priest with local jurisdiction, charged principally with supervising the education given in the schools. Subordinate to these two assistants was the *Ometochtzin,* priest of the god of pulque and the chief of singers.

Priests subordinate to these representatives of a special god were generally called *Tlanamácac.* There were others of lower rank called *Tlamacazqui,* and finally there were the young men called *Tlamacazton,* who served in the temples as novitiates.

There were also major priestesses who were in charge of special cults of the goddess of earth, such as the *Cihuacuacuilli,* and there were still others who served as mother superiors in the convents. Since the migration period of the Aztecs, even before they settled in Tenochtitlán, one of the four leaders of the tribe was a woman called *Chimalma.* Even though she always occupied the lowest rank among the priest-guides, this is proof enough of the importance of priestesses in religious affairs.

In a special building called *Cuicacalli,* sacred music was taught. Two principal priests were in charge of this school of music and of providing everything necessary for this very important part of worship. One was the *Ometochtli,* representative of the god of pulque, and the other, the *Tlapitzcaltzin,* meaning literally "the lord of the house of flutes."

In addition to their ritual functions in connection with the worship of the gods, the priests also had many other duties. The spiritual power that they exercised over Aztec society was enormous, for they were the interpreters of the divinity, and with their rites and ceremonies they could either call down calamity upon the people or bring them prosperity. They also represented the highest culture that an Aztec man could attain, for it can be said that in their possession was all the knowledge that the Mexicans possessed. To be sure, since the planets were gods, the study of astronomy was a sacred subject to which only the representatives of the gods should devote themselves. Hence among the various priestly duties was observation of the celestial movements, not only for scientific-religious ends, but for practical purposes as well, since they must sound the hours on their conch shell trumpets.

Therefore, the calendar with its multiple series and combinations, as well as the prediction of the future, was in their hands. The complicated operations necessary to interpret the *tonalámatl,* the book in which the combinations of the *tonalpohualli* were painted, were the charge of those who were exceptionally skillful, the priests of the goddess Tlazoltéotl.

History and mythology were handed down by word of mouth, aided by the codices, which were, properly speaking, more than simple writing as we now understand it. The codices were a means of recalling events known by memory. It was therefore logical that hieroglyphic writing and its interpretation should also be in the hands of the priests.

Although laws and their enforcement were the province of secular officials, they, too, had all studied in the *Calmécac,* the religious school. War itself was in part a priestly activity, for many of the "satraps," as the chroniclers of the sixteenth century called them, went to war and were given rewards and rank for capturing prisoners.

On the other hand, in medicine, the regular or legally constituted clergy was in sharp competition with the diviners, who, as a result of their ancient practices in magic and their important empirical knowledge of the curative properties of certain plants, could pass themselves off as being endowed with supernatural powers.

The people had great faith in these diviners, more for the unintelligible formulae which they mouthed than for their real knowledge, since these incantations were never pronounced in the common language but rather in "disguised words" *(nahuatlatolli),* the speech peculiar to diviners, or *nahuales.*

Thus it happened that things were not known by their common names. *Chicomoztoc,* which means literally "the seven caves," was the

84

diviner's name for the mouth or the womb. Perhaps this explains why the traditions dealing with the migrations of so many tribes of Meso-america say that these tribes came from Chicomoztoc, that is, from the womb.

Copper was called the "red chichimec," blood was "the red woman," and wood had the calendar name "1 Water." Some expressions, however, are so mysterious that we cannot even venture to guess their meanings. For example, tobacco was called "beaten nine times." Pains were called "serpents" and were of four colors to relate them to the four cardinal points of the compass. There were the blue serpent, the yellow serpent, the red, and the white.

To relieve pains in the shoulder blades, the skin was pricked with a fang of a viper, since like cures like, and then the diviner chanted this conjuration: "Oh thou, blue serpent, yellow serpent, red serpent, or white serpent, cease, for the white and strong pricker has arrived, and he will drive it all off over the mountains and hills; and woe to the one who finds it, for it will destroy him and it will swallow him up."

If one was bitten by a scorpion, it was necessary to invoke the three goddesses—Citlalcueitl, "the lady of the starry skirt"; Chalchiuhtlicue, "the lady of the jade skirt"; and Xochiquetzal—who had conspired to send Xochiquetzal to tempt the penitent Yappan and force him to sin. As punishment for this sin, Yappan was transformed into a scorpion by the gods. After Tezcatlipoca cut off his head, he was transformed into a cricket, given the name of Tzontecomama, "he who bears the head," and sentenced to carry forever and ever the head of Yappan.

Up to the present time, this very important aspect of witchcraft among the ancient Mexicans has had little study. Not only would knowledge of it explain their myths and legends and their concepts of diseases and methods of curing them, but also, of much greater importance, it would give us a better understanding of the indigenous soul than we have at present.

Education was controlled by strict religious principles and was, therefore, imparted by the priests.

The most important school was the *Calmécac* ("row of houses"). Here the children of the nobility were prepared to study the arts and the known sciences. Although the instruction was primarily religious,

85

The great Temple of Tenochtitlán (reconstruction by Miguel Covarrubias).

not all the students in the *Calmécac* were preparing for the priesthood. Many received the type of education which fitted them to occupy other high positions, open only to those who had studied in the *Calmécac*. Education in this school, which was a part of the Great Temple, was extremely rigorous because of the severe discipline to which the students were subjected. It might be said that at the *Calmécac* they underwent a course of training more like that of a monastery than of a school. Not the least important part of this education was training for suffering the privations of war and priestly fasts. Even the sons of great lords had to sleep on the floor, and arise during the night to perform their sacrifices and say their prayers after purifying themselves in any kind of weather in a ritual bath in the pools of the school. They were constantly busy cutting and bringing wood for the sacred fires, gathering maguey leaves, carrying water, sweeping the temples, and making long expeditions at night, wearing no other clothing than the *máxtlatl,* or loin cloth, to reach some far-off corner of the forest where they would deposit in a ball of grass maguey spines stained with their blood and dedicated to the honor of one particular god.

In addition to this school for the nobility, there existed in each district of Tenochtitlán a public school whose primary object was to prepare young men for war. There, discipline was not so severe and the curriculum not so extensive. Nevertheless, a good part of the education consisted of religious practices and acts of penitence and self-sacrifice. These schools were called *Telpochcalli,* "the house of the young men," and in them the majority of the population of Tenochtitlán were educated.

Parents dedicated their children at birth to become priests or warriors. If they wanted the child to be a priest, they would invite the chiefs of the *Calmécac* to a banquet and offer their son to them. The child, if accepted, was taken to the *Calmécac,* where he was painted black and a string of wooden beads called *tlacopatli* hung around his neck. It was thought that the soul of the child was joined to these beads; therefore, before returning the child to his parents, the priests removed the necklace and left it in the monastery as a pledge.

A candidate for the priesthood was enrolled in the *Calmécac* at the age of fifteen and became known as a *tlamacazton.* He was then initiated into the harsh routine of work, discipline, and abstinence. It

87

was necessary for him to be very careful, for if he broke or stained any object entrusted to his care, a fine was imposed which the parents had to pay. If they failed to pay the fine at the proper time, he was punished by being thrown into the lagoon and beaten until he was senseless. If he committed a grave mistake, he was expelled from the *Calmécac*.

Later, the youth, now trained, helped the priest in the rites of the cult. He carried the sacrificial instruments, he played the *teponaztli* or wooden drum, and he watched the stars in order to sound the hour. He was taught songs dedicated to the gods, along with writing and sacerdotal painting, astrology, history, the calculation of the days and the years, and the interpretation of dreams.

During his novitiate he must remain celibate, and he was severely punished if any violation of this rule was discovered. He could, however, marry as soon as he left the *Calmécac,* even though he was to be a priest.

When the army went to war, it was accompanied by armed priests, and the young men of the *Calmécac* carried their gear. Both the priests and the *tlamacazton* fought the enemy and took prisoners, receiving thereby medals and compensation. By this time the novice could paint on his face a red semicircle, reaching from his temples to his chin, which was a distinctive sacerdotal marking.

After having distinguished himself in war or in religious practices, the youth entered upon a career in the army or the priesthood, the judiciary or the government, according to his inclination, and was promoted on his merits or according to his lineage.

There were other special schools, as has been said, which taught dancing, singing, and playing musical instruments, but all this instruction had primarily a religious purpose.

Naturally, to carry out the complex duties assigned and to attend to the complicated rituals of the many gods, a large number of priests, teachers, singers, and novices was necessary. Torquemada[1] says that

---

[1] Juan de Torquemada (?-1625), a Franciscan friar of Spanish origin, who came to Mexico as a child. He took the habit of St. Francis and later served as provincial of his order. In 1609 he was ordered by the Commissioner General of the Indies to write his *Monarquia Indiana*. The work was finished in 1613. In three parts, it deals with the antiquities of New Spain, Cortés' expedition, religion and customs of the Indians, and the evangelization of the natives.

88

five thousand persons were employed in the service of the Great Temple alone, and that each *calpulli,* or district of the city, also had temples dedicated to its local deities.

Although some of the services that these priests performed were without doubt of prime importance to the community, their enormous number must have been a great burden on the food-producing part of the population, for it was impossible for the latter to do any work not related to maintaining the worship of the gods or the waging of war for religious or political purposes.

A priest who went to war *(Codex Mendocino 65).*

THE PEOPLE OF THE SUN

FROM THIS brief description, the tremendous role that religion played among the Aztecs can be realized. It was so great that it is no exaggeration to say that their entire existence revolved around their religion and that there was not a single act, public or private, that was not tinged by religious sentiment.

Religion was the preponderant factor, and provided the basis even of those activities which appear most alien to religious sentiment, such as sports, games, and war. Religion regulated commerce, politics, and conquest, and intervened in every event in the individual's life, from the time he was born until the priests burned his corpse and buried his ashes. It was the prime motive for all individual acts and was the basic reason for the existence of the state itself.

We can define the Aztec political organization as a military theocracy in which the warrior was subordinate to the priest and the emperor himself, or, more properly, the *Tlacatecuhtli,* was a priest, for he and all the high officials of state had been educated in the sacerdotal school, the *Calmécac.*

Just as religion played a preponderant role in the political organization, it was also dominant in the social organization, for the clans, or *calpullis*—which word the Spaniards translated into *barrios,* or districts of a city—were not territorial divisions, except as they were under the patronage of a particular god and were the continuation of old families bound not by a biological tie, but by a spiritual kinship which originated in the common worship of a patron god.

This makes it evident why the elders of each city district had a very direct influence on the private lives of the individual families and why they were consulted about marriages, the enrollment of children in schools or in the army, or any matter of solemn or important consequence.

What is the explanation of this omnipresence of religion? We cannot understand it if we do not comprehend that the individual Aztec felt that his people were a people with a mission, a people elected by

90

The founding of Tenochtitlán *(Durán atlas, 3).*

the tribal god to carry out the destiny of the world and realize the human ideal as they understood it.

The Aztecs were the people of the sun; their city, Tenochtitlán, was founded on the site where the eagle, the representative of Huitzilopochtli, alighted on the stone cactus in the middle of the island in the Lake of the Moon. This lake was Lake Texcoco, known esoterically as Meztliapan. There the heart of the first sacrificial victim was thrown. There the tree of thorns was to spring forth, the tree of sacrifice which symbolized the place of thorns, *Huitztlampa,* the land of the sun, the place to which the tribe had migrated from their home in the white land, Aztlán.

Their priests, the leaders of the migration, had told them that when the sun, represented by an eagle, should alight upon a spiny cactus whose red tunas were like human hearts, there, in that place only, were they to rest and found a city. For this meant that the people of the sun, the chosen people of Huitzilopochtli, had arrived at the place where they were to grow great and become the masters of the world, where they were to become the instrument through which the god would accomplish great deeds. Therefore, the god spoke to them in this fashion:

91

In truth I will lead thee to the place to which thou art to go; I will appear in the guise of a white eagle; wherever thou art to go, there will I go crying unto thee; go then, watching me only, and when I arrive there, I will alight and there thou wilt see me; so presently make my temple, my home, my bed of grass, there where I was lifted up to fly, and there the people shall make their home, there wilt thou establish thyself.

The first thing to adorn thee shall be the order of the eagle, the order of the jaguar, the sacred war, arrow and shield; this is what thou shalt eat, what thou shalt be needing; and so thou shalt go striking terror. As a reward for thy valor, thou shalt conquer and destroy all the plebeians and the settlers who are already established there, as soon as thou seest the site.

And the god offered the conquerors and brave men the wrought mantles, the *maxtles,* the tail-feathers of the quetzal bird, to be their emblems and their coat of arms, and they would receive "all things in general: the good, the placid, the fragrant flowers, tobacco, and song, whatever things there be."

In like manner was I sent on this mission, and I was charged to bring arms, bow, arrows, and shield. My principal purpose in coming and my vocation is war, and likewise with my breast, my head, and my arms I must see after and carry on my vocation in many cities and among the peoples which there are today.

First, I shall conquer in war in order to have and name my home of precious emerald and gold, decorated with featherwork. The house shall be adorned with precious emerald as transparent as crystal, and I shall also have all kinds of precious heads of corn, chocolate, cotton, and cloth of many colors, and I shall have it all to see and to possess, for it is commanded of me and my office and for that purpose I came.

And in Coatepec he had told them:

Behold, Mexicans, here is to be your responsibility and your vocation, here you are to watch and wait, and from all four corners of the earth, you are to conquer, earn, and subdue for yourselves. Have then body, breast, head, arms, and strength, for it likewise will cost much sweat, work, and pure blood for you to obtain and enjoy the fine emeralds, precious stones, gold, silver, fine featherwork, rare feathers of all colors, fine chocolate brought from afar, cotton of different hues, many sweet-smelling flowers, all manner of different delicious, delicate fruits, and many other things bringing great pleasure and contentment.

The people of the sun, led by the priests of the god, settled in the middle of the Lake of the Moon. Then they began to fulfill their mission by collaborating in the cosmic function through human sacrifice, a symbolic representation of the assistance that man must give to the sun so that the latter can continue his struggle against the moon and the stars and vanquish them every day.

Each prisoner taken by the Aztecs was a star that was to be sacrificed to the sun to nourish him with the magical sustenance that represents life and to fortify him for the divine combat. The man-star who was sacrificed had his body painted white and wore a black mask signifying the star-studded night. It was believed that he would reinforce with his life the life of the sun.

Hence the pride of the Aztec, who looked upon himself as a collaborator of the gods, for he knew that his life was dedicated to maintaining cosmic order and struggling against the powers of darkness.

In a sense the universe depended upon him for its continued existence; upon him depended the food for the gods, upon him depended the beneficence of the gifts which they showered on mankind. Likewise, the light of the sun, the rain that formed in the mountains and watered the corn, the wind that blew through the reeds, bringing clouds or turning into a hurricane, all depended upon him.

But since the Aztec was a soldier of the sun, and since he had this divine mission in life, to him also went the rewards. To him should belong "things in general, the good, the placid, the fragrant flowers, tobacco, and song."

It is evident that the Aztecs, like every people who believe they have a mission, were better prepared to fulfill that mission if their conquest of other peoples was based upon a manifest destiny. Since the sixteenth century, the apostolic and civilizing zeal of the European peoples has been fired to an extraordinary degree, especially when they feel called upon to save the wealthy from the "barbarians," and more particularly so when those riches cannot be obtained in "civilized" coun-

93

tries: gold, spices, and pearls in the sixteenth century; petroleum, rubber, coal, henequen, and cinchona in the twentieth century.

The Aztecs, like all imperialistic peoples, always found justification for their conquests, to extend the dominion of the city-state, Tenochtitlán, and to convert the king of Mexico into the king of the world, known as *Cem-Anáhuac tlatoani,* and Mexico-Tenochtitlán into the capital of the empire which they called *Cem-Anáhuac tenochca tlalpan,* or "the land of the Tenochcas." The idea that they were collaborators of the gods, the concept that they were fulfilling a transcendental duty and that on their action rested the possibility that the world might continue to exist, enabled the Aztecs to undergo the hardships of their migrations, to settle in a place that the richest and most advanced peoples had rejected, and to subjugate their neighbors. Hence they kept up a constant expansion of their territorial conquests, until their leaders had carried the power of Tenochtitlán to the Atlantic and Pacific coasts, and had subjected to their domination the more advanced and older peoples who were in possession of the lands on the high plateaus and the coasts.

In addition to this cosmological ideal, the Aztecs also believed that they had an ethical ideal to attain. The struggle of the sun against the powers of darkness was not only a struggle of the gods, but it was also, above all, the struggle of good against evil. The mission of the Aztecs, was, then, to be on the side of the sun, the symbol of good, opposing the fearful gods of darkness, the symbols of evil.

Consequently, the Aztecs had to carry on this ethical struggle until their divine leader should succeed in defeating the evil gods who plotted the destruction of man, and until man should likewise triumph over the powers of evil, symbolic of sin. This concept of sin included primarily drunkenness and sexual incontinence, but the gravest sin was failure to participate in the divine plan, that is, failure to fulfill one's duties toward the gods, or, in other words, to show fear in combat.

As a result, the fundamental virtue among this religious, warlike people was courage displayed in combat and stoicism in the face of pain or death. Even the *macegual,* or common people, could acquire rank through merit, and the king could make them nobles by bestowing knighthood upon them.

Opposed to this imperialistic and religious ideal there was always

94

a feeling of pessimism in the depths of the Aztec soul. The Aztecs knew that in the end their leader, the sun, would be defeated and would have to perish amidst fearful earthquakes, and then the powers of evil would prevail. The stars and the planets, led by the moon, would descend to the earth, but no longer by means of the tenuous thread of spider web on which, from time to time, during the days of evil fortune, the *tzitzimime* came down. Instead, they would descend from the heavens in innumerable squadrons of fierce beasts and would destroy mankind.

Therefore, this life, for the Aztecs, was only transitory, and a feeling of pessimism and anguish appeared in their vigorous and terrible sculpture and a tinge of profound sadness in their poetry.

> *We only came to sleep,*
> *We only came to dream,*
> *It is not true, no, it is not true*
> *That we came to live on the earth.*
>
> *We are changed into the grass of springtime;*
> *Our hearts will grow green again*
> *And they will open their petals,*
> *But our body is like a rose tree:*
> *It puts forth flowers and then withers.*

This profound melancholy contrasts sharply with the energetic concept of being a chosen people, and here is the fundamental contradiction in the Aztec culture.

But if religion was for the Aztecs the strength and reason of their lives, if it took them from the coast of one ocean to another and made Tenochtitlán the queen of Anáhuac, it was also a fatal limitation for their culture, as, on a minor scale, it was for all the indigenous cultures of Mexico and Central America.

The creative force of a youthful people was, of necessity, concentrated in the production of religious works. In art as well as in science, in the political and social organization, and in the philosophy of life, the religion that had acted as an incentive became a restraint, and the products of religious enthusiasm smothered the creative personality of the individual and destroyed all possibilities of cultural development.

95

The bundle of the dead (*Codex Magliabecchiano* 57).

When the Conquest took them by surprise, the Aztecs were still a semicivilized people who had not yet reached the cultural refinement of the Mayas, the Toltecs, the Totonacs, or the Mixtecs. The Aztecs were in the midst of a flourishing era, but the old indigenous cultures that had already disappeared are eloquent proof of the sterility in which those great civilizations finally ended. They had lacked a constantly progressive ideal that would have led them to conceive of life as something more than an invariable, meticulous repetition of ceremonies in honor of the gods.

Among the great cultures of Mesoamerica, religion, in great part, took the place of technical invention. The fundamental belief was that man did not have to solve his own problems, but must implore the gods to solve them and take pity on mankind. For the Indians of Mesoamerica, sacrifice was the technical means that made the rain fall, the corn grow, an illness disappear, a father, husband, or son return safe from an expedition of war or commerce, or a wife give birth to a strong, vigorous

96

child. Man alone could do nothing; his technique was ineffectual. Only by sacrifice could he induce the gods to satisfy with benevolence the needs of mankind.

This profound religiosity of the Mexican Indian, still very much in evidence today, is the scarlet thread in the woof of history; it allows us to understand his way of life, at times indolent, at times active and energetic, but always stoic, because the life of man, according to his way of thinking, depends on the impenetrable will of the gods.

PHOTOGRAPHS

The Stone of the Suns. Above, left, the Sun of the Tiger; right, the Sun of Water. Below, left, the Sun of Fire; right, the Sun of Air. *National Museum of Mexico.*

The Aztec Calendar, or Stone of the Sun. *National Museum of Mexico.*

The battle of the Eagles and the Jaguars—a *huehuetl* (a vertical cylindrical drum with a skin head) from Malinalco. *Museum of Toluca.*

Tláloc. *Echániz Collection.*

Chalchiuhtlicue. *National Museum of Mexico.*

Chicomolotzin, serpent with seven ears of corn. *National Museum of Mexico.*

Chicomecóatl, or
"Seven Serpent."
National Museum of Mexico.

Xochipilli.
*National Museum
of Mexico.*

[VIII]

Xipe Tótec. *Salomón Hale Collection.*

Tlaltecuhtli's hair, relief on a *cuauhxicalli,* or "eagle vase."
National Museum of Mexico.

The great Coatlicue. *National Museum of Mexico*.

Yolotlicue.
National Museum of Mexico.

Cihuateteo. *National Museum of Mexico.*

Owl on a *cuauhxicalli,* or "eagle vase." *National Museum of Mexico.*

A sacrificial knife. *Reproduced through the courtesy of the British Museum.*

The *Volador* (flying game), according to Clavijero.

Knight of the Order of the Eagle.
National Museum of Mexico.

INDEX

Acecentli (water corn), in story of creation: 15f.
Acocentli (pine nuts), food of early man: 15f.
Acolnahuácatl (god of death): 64
Agave: *see* maguey
Ajolote (salamander): *see* Axólotl
Aldebaran (star), and ceremony of earthquake: 20
Alligator: as representative of earth, 10; in calendar, 33, 65f.; earth as, 52
Alvarado, Pedro de: 77 & n., 78
Amate: 44
Amulets, as help to souls in underworld: 62
Anáhuac: 95
Átlatl, dart hurler: 31
Atlatonan, marriage of warrior to: 69
Atlixco: 11
Atltlachinolli, "water, a burned thing": 36
Auianime, lived with bachelor warriors: 47
Axólotl (salamander), in creation of sun: 18
Aztatzontli (feather headdress): 43
Aztaxelli (ornament): 31
Aztecs: rise of, *xiii;* origin of, *xiii;* civilization of, *xiii*ff.; settlement of in Mexico, *xiv;* capital of, *xv;* end of civilization of, *xv;* modern descendants of ancient, *xvi;* as chosen people of sun, 13–14; ages of, 16; complexity of gods, 23–26; myths of as explanations, 31; calendars of, 31–33, 39, 65–81; mythical home of, 34; maguey used by, 47–48; pantheon of, 51; earth gods of, 52–56; art of, 53; religion of, 54; cult of, 56; underworld of, 56, 60–65; astrologers of, 66–67; and human sacrifice, 72–74; priests of, 81–89; importance of religion among, 90–97; as soldiers of sun, 93; justification of for conquest, 93–94; virtues and sins of, 94; pessimism of, 94–95; poetry of, 95
Aztlán: 91; Tenochca Aztecs from, *xiv*

Ball: game of, 79; religious significance of, 80
Bat, associated with death: 56–58
Bering Strait: *xiii*
Berlin Museum of Ethnography: 43
Birds: men changed into, 15; in creation, 16; plumage of for mosaics, 25

Blood, human: nourishment of gods with 12; maguey spines dyed in, 17; offering of, 36; pricked from ears, 67; spilling of in sacrifice, 73
Bolivia, Incas in: *xiv*

Calendar name: 7; of Chalchiuhtlicue, 44; significance of, 45
Calendars: 54; division of by four cardinal points, 11; man taught to arrange, 25; advanced form of, 31–33; signs of, 65; festivals of, 67–72; favorable days of, 67ff.; agricultural, 68; rituals of, 72–81; in charge of priests, 84
Calmécac, religious school: 84; patron of, 29; instruction in, 85–88; entrance into, 87; expulsion from, 88; education of state officials in, 90
Calpulli (clan of merchants): 67, 89; temple of, 68; formed by spiritual kinship, 90
Camaxtle, tutelar god: 10, 37; *see also* Tezcatlipoca
Cannibalism, as religious ceremony: 74–75
Castillo, Bernal Díaz del, impressions of Aztec capital: *xv*
Ce Ácatl (year 1519): 25
Cem-Anáhuac tenochca tlalpan, capital of the world: 94
Cem-Anáhuac tlatoani, king of the world: 94
Cempoala, priests of: 83
Cencocopi, ancestor of corn: food of early man, 15; as ideal food, 16
Centéotl (god of corn): 46; son of Tlazoltéotl, 54; song to, 76
Centli (corn): 46; *see also* corn
Central America: 25; Aztecs' entrance in, *xiii;* development of civilization in, *xv;* ritual calendar in, 10; Aztec culture inherited from, 11; food of, 16; organized cults of, 17; veneration of Quetzalcóatl in, 26; ancient gods of, 27; god of fire in, 38; cultures in, 41; calendars in, 66; early ball game in, 79; words for migrations in, 85; religion of, 95
Centzonhuitznáhuac (the stars): 13, 37
Centzon Mimixcoa (stars of the north): 41

endar, 33; and gods of death, 53; in sculpture, 54; in calendar, 65ff.; as word for pain, 85
Serpent of fire, in legend of Huitzilopochtli: 13
Seven, significance of number: 46
Shoshonis, relation of to Aztecs: *xiv*
Sky, held up by Quetzalcóatl: 15
Songs, as religious ritual: 75–76
South America, Aztecs in: *xiii*
Spaniards, arrival of: *xv*
Spider, associated with death: 58
Stars: in legend of Coatlicue, 13; man studies movements of, 25; worship of, 37; mother of, 53; in second heaven, 65
Sun: in Huitzilopochtli cult, 12–14; creation of, 14–15, 17–20; worship of, 31–36; and paradise, 58; in third heaven, 65; ceremony of, 67; people of, 90–97

Tabasco: 26
Tajín, Totonac rain god: 41
Tamales, in festival of Xocotlhuetzi: 71
Tarascans: *xiv,* 74
Téchcatl (sacrificial stone): victims of in paradise, 58; use of, 73
Tecólotl (owl): 58
Telpochcalli: school of war for plebians, 29; education in, 87
Telpochtli, "he who never grows old": 27
Tenayuca: temple at, 33, 83; pyramid of, 39
Tenochca, migration of: *xiv*
Tenochtitlán: 34, 83, 91; settlement of, *xiv;* worship in, 28; Great Temple of, 33; founding of, 36; flowers in, 47; ball courts at, 80; priests of, 83; schools in, 87; extension of dominion of, 94; queen of Anáhuac, 95; *see also* Mexico City
Teotihuacán: 25; religious center at, *xiv;* gods of, 8; meeting of gods in, 17; culture of, 38, 49; god Tláloc in, 41; paintings from, 60; calendar of, 66
Teocentli, ancestor of corn: 15f.; *see also cencocopi*
Teomama, spokesmen of god: 35
Téotl (god): 46
Teotleco, month of: 29, 38
Teoyaomiqui (god of the enemy dead): 59
Tepanteohuatzin, priests in charge of education: 83
Tepeyolohtli (god of mountains): 21, 29

Teponaztli, wooden drum in religious rites: 88
Tepoztécatl (wine god): 7; myths about, 48
Tepoztlán, Morelos: 7; myths told in, 48
Teteoinan (mother of gods): 53; *see also* Coatlicue
Texcoco: 8; worship in, 28
Texcoco, Lake: 91
Tezcapoctli (shining smoke): 28
Tezcatlipoca (creator god): 38; as god of evil, 26; meaning of name, 27–28; functions of, 27–29; names of, 28–29; description of, 29–31; as god of fire, 39; steals wife of Tláloc, 42; kidnaps Xochiquetzal, 47; and Xipe, 51; festivals for, 68; and human sacrifice, 72; in legend of scorpion, 85
Tizatlán, paintings on altars of: 11
Tlacatecuhtli, and priestly functions of: 81–82, 90
Tlachtli (court for ball game): 79
Tlacochtli (darts): 31
Tlacopatli (string of beads): 87
Tlahuicole, warrior in gladiatorial sacrifice: 73–74
Tlahuizcalpantecuhtli "lord of the house of dawn": twofold form of, 24; as astral deity, 37
Tláloc (god of rain and celestial fire): 45; in creation of sun, 15; wife of carried off, 29; in calendar, 33; legend of, 41–42; as mountain range, 42; representations of, 42–43; festivals for, 68; songs to, 75; priest of, 82
Tlalocan, paradise of Tláloc: 60
Tlalocatecuhtli (god of water), legend of: 41–42
Tlaltecuhtli: 53
Tlaltetalco, settlement of: *xiv*
Tlamacazqui, subordinate priests: 83
Tlamacazton, candidate for priesthood: 87–88; part of in war, 88
Tlanamácac, subordinate priests: 83
Tlapitzcaltzin, "lord of house of flutes": 83
Tlatoani: see Tlacatecuhtli
Tlaxcala: 10f., 15, 42
Tlaxcaltecans: as special challengers, 14; warrior of in gladiatorial combat, 73
Tlazoltéotl (goddess of filth): 53; appearance of, 54; priests of, 56, 84
Tlecuil, brazier as center of home: 38
Tlemaitl (incense pots): 38

THE AZTECS

follows closely the design and spirit of the original Mexican edition. The text is set in 14 point Granjon with two points of space between lines. Granjon, designed by George W. Jones in 1924, is an adaptation of the classic Garamond types. The book has been printed by offset in six colors of ink. The drawings were reproduced from the original line color separations by Miguel Covarrubias and represent in their full authenticity and beauty some of the last of that great Mexican artist's work. Unfortunately, the art work for the black line plates of *the bearded Quetzal-cóatl, the dead Sun, gladiatorial sacrifice, the Aztec dance,* and *the founding of Tenochtitlán* had been lost and had to be redrawn. Richard Palmer of the University of Oklahoma Press staff supplied these by working from the remaining plates of the drawings and by careful comparison with the Mexican edition.

 UNIVERSITY OF OKLAHOMA PRESS : NORMAN

DATE DUE

MAY 5 '71	APR 26 '78		
MAY 26 '71	NOV 29 '78		
OCT 26 '71	APR 2 5		
NOV 8 '71	MAY 2		
NOV 29 '71	NOV 2 8		
OCT 30 '72	MAY 0 1 1980		
	MAY 1 1985		
NOV 26 '74	MAY 1 1 1988		
FEB 4 '75			
MAY 2 '75			
NOV 1 '75			
DEC 3 '75			
DEC 18 '75			
APR 28 '76			
NOV 22 '76			
MAR 21 '77			
MAY 5 '78			